HOLLOW FAITH

How Andy Griffith, Facebook, and the American Dream Diluted the Gospel

Stephen Ingram

HOLLOW FAITH:
HOW ANDY GRIFFITH, FACEBOOK, AND THE AMERICAN DREAM DILUTED THE GOSPEL

Youth Ministry Partners and Abingdon Press.

Copyright © 2015 by Stephen Ingram

All rights reserved.

Library of Congress Cataloging-in-Publication Data

CIP Data has been requested.

15 16 17 18 19 20 21 22 23 24—10 9 8 7 6 5 4 3 2 1

MANUFACTURED IN THE UNITED STATES OF AMERICA

CONTENTS

ACKNOWLEDGMENTS

It is so important to thank the people who have shaped, loved and guided me in this literary journey, but more importantly in my life's journey.

There are a series of mentors, Rev. Dudley Rose, Seth Coleman, Dr. Graham Walker, Dr. Paul Holloway, the late Dr. John Claypool and Dr. Dennis Sansom, whom I hope can find pieces of themselves and their profound influence on me throughout these pages. My great appreciation also goes to Mark DeVries, to whom I cannot adequately express my gratefulness for being such an important mentor, guide, and friend. I also want to thank my comrades in ministry Paul, Robin, Mike, Bill, Warren, Drew, Annie, and Rachel for graciously indulging and caring for me on an everyday basis as we minister together. So many of the insights and positive understandings of ministry have also come from the students of Canterbury Student Ministry and the loving and gracious congregation at Canterbury United Methodist Church. Thanks to my family, my uncle and aunt Dr. Benjamin and Sandra Ingram; my mother and father-in-law, John and Laurie Moses; and my sister, Meagan Morrow, for their love, kindness, guidance and constant support.

Finally, this book is dedicated to my family. To my three, beautiful children—Mary Clare, Patrick, and Nora Grace—I envision for you a faith and life that is sincere, authentic, robust, and world changing. I hope that you will choose peace over violence, love over hate, and hope over fear. You are so wonderful and beautiful, and I am so thankful for each of you. To my wife, partner, and friend, Mary Liz, this journey is only beginning; let us travel forward, grateful for the road behind us, joyous for the horizon ahead. My deep and undying love to you all.

FOREWORD

Rather than a tired rehashing of soon-to-be-outdated statistics or a repackaging of the same old youth ministry themes, *Hollow Faith* awakens us to a view of youth ministry with a wider lens, one based on the reality of how the faith of next generation is being shaped (or not, which is too often the case). This is a book that separates the values of the gospel from the cultural norms that have domesticated them, norms like politeness, patriotism, and entertainment.

This book holds the promise of reframing our understanding of the most crucial challenges facing youth ministry today. Stephen's evocative metaphors—like pancake spirituality, the myth of Mayberry, and the cell phone as the extended umbilical cord—may just find their way to awaken sleeping churches and realign us with the core truths of the gospel.

For the past decade, there has probably been no study more frequently quoted in the field of youth ministry than the *National Study of Youth and Religion*. We have been waiting for an accessible resource to translate these findings of the 346-page sociological report into a format that can be used with our volunteer leaders, our students and their parents. And Stephen, through the Center for Youth Ministry Training, has provided us with just such a resource.

Hollow Faith is not just a book to be read but to be enacted. The first part of the book is provocative and thorough, but I am even more excited about what comes after: six sessions for parents (and six sessions for youth, included with your purchase of this book and downloadable at *youthministrymartners.com/hollowfaith*), designed to help unpack the difficult-to-grasp results of the National Study of Youth and Religion.

Over the past few years, through my work with Youth Ministry Architects, I've had the privilege of watching the evolving contours of Stephen's ministry. Each time I meet with him as his coach, I find myself taking notes. When he recommends a book, I read it. When he points me to an app, I download it. And more than once, I have found my own ministry impacted by what I learn while coaching Stephen. Like any champion, Stephen simply refuses to stop learning.

On more than one occasion, I've referred to Stephen Ingram as the "Steve Jobs of the Youth Ministry world." I'm hard pressed to recall anyone with the inventiveness and informed creativity of this young man. His laboratory has been his own ministry, where the principles of this book were formed, week-in and week-out in the rough-and-tumble reality of dancing with the alligators of church work, where simple answers never work.

Don't be surprised if you don't agree, at least initially, with everything Stephen writes. His writing is challenging, inviting us to shake free from the assumed answers about youth ministry and the easy compartmentalization that has become so normal in the Christian church in the U.S. As unsettling as these words can be, I also found them to be balanced and fair, with Stephen offering balanced treatment of more touchy subjects.

At a past youth ministry convention, I had the chance to sit with some of my favorite youth ministry sages when our conversation turned to one of my favorite topics.

We wondered out loud, "What are we geezers in youth ministry doing to encourage and raise up young voices who will shape the conversations 20 or 30 years from now?"

Stephen's is a voice I'm thrilled to introduce to you. Though this may be his first book, I doubt it will be the last of his that you'll be reading!

—*Mark DeVries*

INTRODUCTION

HOLLOW

Our Dirty Little Secret

Most youth ministers have a dirty little secret. It is one that we believe will get us fired if too many people find out about it. Most are scared to tell parents or volunteers, and many even fear telling their pastors. It is shocking. Its disquieting nature would rock the very foundation of the churches we serve and has the potential to split our congregations in half. We know this secret, the harm it causes; and yet most of us have perpetuated it for much of our careers. Many of us are scared to disclose this secret because of how intertwined we are in its scandalous tentacles. I am writing this book to finally tell that secret, to liberate all of us who know the secret but are unable to say it ourselves.

We believe that the church is failing.

We believe that the church is producing poor imitations of Christianity.

We see the hollow, disconnected faith of its people.

We see youth disengaging, we know why, and we know that no one wants to hear the truth.

But we also know that we simply cannot wait any longer.

The Research and the Practice

It is interesting how many youth ministers sense, deep in their gut, that the message of Jesus we see in the Bible is just not matching up with the faith so many seem to be practicing. Many of us were and are sometimes dismissed as young, idealistic, and irrational for believing that this could be different. Over time, many of us succumb to the belief that "this is just how the faith operates." We sometimes recite the platitudes of "people are broken" and "none of us are perfect" as excuses for the watered-down versions of the faith we see being practiced and that we often are practicing ourselves. Through all of this, many of us still have an itch, a longing for something more. Christianity just does not seem, well, Christian. We know that this form of the faith is too easy, too nice, too hollow. When we read the Gospels, we see a bright, vibrant faith that actually changed lives. I'm not talking about changes such as "I don't use swear words anymore" or "I now go to church every Sunday." In the Gospels, we see full life changes, like dropping everything, rejecting cultural norms, and following Jesus no matter the repercussions. We see people regularly going against the government, family, and friends because they knew that they answered to a higher authority. We see a gritty, raw faith, full of life, vibrancy, and creativity. We see this Christianity in the Gospels; but for many of us, it is absent in our churches.

In 2003, Wave 1 of a massive study was released, called the National Study of Youth and Religion (NSYR), which added data to support our suspicions. The study hones in on the faith of the American teenager. It is a comprehensive (3,000 interviews) study endowed by the Lilly Foundation and directed by sociologist Christian Smith that attempts to find the religious underpinnings of the spirituality and faith of teenagers. For many, its results are shocking; for most practitioners, it put insightful and concise language to the realities we see every day in our youth ministries. The study has hundreds of observations about what is important to young people's faith, how they practice it, and its lack of staying power into adulthood. These observations were boiled down into three simple but loaded words: Moralistic Therapeutic Deism (MTD). This MTD is the faith that Christian Smith concludes that the majority of American teenagers practice.

Smith and his team wrote the following five statements of belief that characterize the faith of the average teenager:

1. "A god exists who created and ordered the world and watches over human life on earth."
2. "God wants people to be good, nice, and fair to each other, as taught in the Bible and by most world religions."
3. "The central goal of life is to be happy and to feel good about oneself."
4. "God does not need to be particularly involved in one's life, except when God is needed to resolve a problem."
5. "Good people go to heaven when they die."[1]

Written more simply, the average teenager's belief can be summed up as "the importance of being nice, feeling good about yourself, and saving God for emergencies."[2]

This study and its results provided a framework by which to better and more critically analyze the predominant faith of American teenagers. When the NSYR came out, there was much talk and panic about the state of youth ministry and its "failure." Still, many of us knew that there was more going on than just too much "Chubby Bunny" and lock-ins with no purpose. Many felt that we were only scratching the surface of the problem. Kenda Creasy

Dean, Professor of Youth, Church and Culture at Princeton Theological Seminary, was one of those people.

While *Hollow Faith* is not about Dean's groundbreaking book *Almost Christian,* her findings provide great nuance to the method of this book and how I interact with Christian Smith's work. Dean's most prolific game-changing contribution to the discussion was that while the NSYR was about the faith of the American teenager, it actually painted a much broader picture of the faith of the parents of these youth, as well as the church in general. Her analysis and conclusions show us that the faith of our youth is a mirror of the faith of their parents. She not only pointed out the mirror effect but also reminded us that this inconsequential faith is less than appealing and, consequentially, is being abandoned by teenagers everywhere. This understanding heavily influenced how I chose to write this book. Instead of dealing with only youth culture trends, I chose to look at our culture at large, focusing at times on primarily adult religious culture. This added focus is why you will find discussions of Joel Osteen and others in this book: It's not that I believe that our youth watch Osteen, but I do know that their parents are indirectly, if not directly, influenced by this type of religious trend.

Dean's emphasis on the primacy of the parents' role in their children's spirituality is also the basis for the second half of the book, where I provide a series of parent/family lessons and activities about the six concepts of *Hollow Faith.* I hope this to be a work that will translate much of the thickness of the NSYR into very practical and applicable terms for the average student minister wanting to see, develop, and nurture real and consequential faith in his or her youth. I also hope that this book will broaden the understanding of the youth minister, pastor, parent, and volunteer to understand that the term *youth ministry* is a misnomer. There is no such thing as only ministry to youth; it has to be understood as ministry to youth, parents, families, grandparents, and the entire body of Christ.

MIRROR, MIRROR ON THE WALL

Being Honest With Our Reflections

One of the primary methods I used in writing this book was to look deeply into the mirror of pop culture and try to ask the difficult, and often maddening, questions of the self as defined through those things we produce and consume. This exploration into pop culture added another set of observations to the book you have in your hands. The first three chapters focus primarily on Smith's three categories of the average teenager's faith: Moralistic, Therapeutic and Deistic. I work through his research, drawing out the most practical applications. The next three chapters are based on three other resounding themes in our culture as reflected in youth, understood as Meism, Consumerism, and Pluralism. I explore these themes through the lenses of pop culture as well as current sociological and psychological data.

I chose Andy Griffith, Facebook, and the American Dream as sort of meta examples of the six observations explored in this book. I think of them as:

- How we believe we should act (*The Andy Griffith Show*);

- How we want to be known (Facebook); and

- What we aspire to become (The American Dream).

Wrapped up in these three are the underlying foundational principles of Moralism, Therapeutic Religion, Modern Deism, Self-Absorption (meism), Consumerism, and a nationalistic/nativist-flavored response to the cultural resurgence of Pluralism. While there are other examples of these trends, the three I chose seem to be the most all-encompassing and descriptive of the overarching cumulative portrait of religion in America.

A Holistic Approach

I've taken a holistic approach to the material. It is academic, practical, theoretical, functional, curriculum, guide, discussion-starter, and manual. When deciding on the format, I did not want to paint myself into a corner of purely academic thought; I knew, while it had to take seriously and engage the academic piece (part one of the book), to leave it there would not completely fulfill my or the Lilly Endowment's goal. I also wanted to be intentional in engaging with the findings of Dean's *Almost Christian*. In writing this book, I knew that youth group could not be the only medium in which to convey these messages. To not include a strong parent piece would not only defeat much of the purpose of the book, but would also work opposite of what we are (re)discovering to be the primary place of spiritual nurture: the home. For these reasons the second part of this book is a parent/family piece. Finally, I also wanted to give tools to the youth minister, in order to practically translate the material into a form, such as small groups, that would challenge the students. To accomplish this aim, this book comes with a downloadable six-session youth curriculum based on the six findings discussed previously.

This book is meant to be read by youth ministers and pastors; it should be read by parents and volunteers as well. It is a tool to recognize serious shifts in our faith and to act as a sort of starting point from which to have discussions, develop plans, and form actions to reclaim the vibrant, life-giving faith of the Bible. This book is meant to be accessible and inviting, critical, and hopeful. A youth minister who reads this book alone, outside of the community of his or her pastor, parents, and volunteers will not be able to fully utilize its findings or its methods. This is a book meant for churches as a whole, not just youth groups trying to recover their faith. Finally, this book is meant to be a catalyst. It is not a period in the discussion; it is one small interjection into a much larger dialogue that is ongoing and should continue to grow, working to reshape faith in the American church. For too long we have shaped the Gospel until it is now a shell of its bold former self.

Rediscovering the Gospel That Reads Us

"Apply yourself closely to the text; Apply the text closely to yourself."—Dr. Peter J. Gomes, *The Good Book*

I spent nine years in higher theological education, with the purpose of learning how to "read" the Bible. Through dozens of courses in biblical interpretation and theology, and by honing my understanding of the historical-critical method, I gained a much greater understanding and appreciation for this unique text. One of the things I discovered during my time studying and dissecting the text was that I had become very good at reading the Bible.

I had not become as good at letting the Bible read me.

I had been trained to interpret the text in its historical context, and even better at reinterpreting it and applying it to the everyday lives of our youth. I could tell you, with some confidence and reasoning, what Jesus was saying to his contemporaries, to youth, and to the Church. I had become less confident at understanding what the text was saying to me, and even more so what the text was saying about me.

One of the most important lessons I try to teach my youth today is that the primary purpose of the gospel is not being a gospel for us to interpret and apply to life. It is a document that should be applied and allowed to interpret us, our beliefs, communities, nations, vices, and virtues. The gospel is not our tool for living; it is the standard by which we measure how we live. I hope that we can rediscover this gospel that reads us.

1. *Soul Searching : The Religious and Spiritual Lives of American Teenagers,* by Christian Smith, pages 162–163.
2. *Soul Searching,* Smith, pages 162–163.

Download the *Hollow Faith* youth curriculum, included with your purchase of this book, at

http://youthministrymartners.com/hollowfaith.

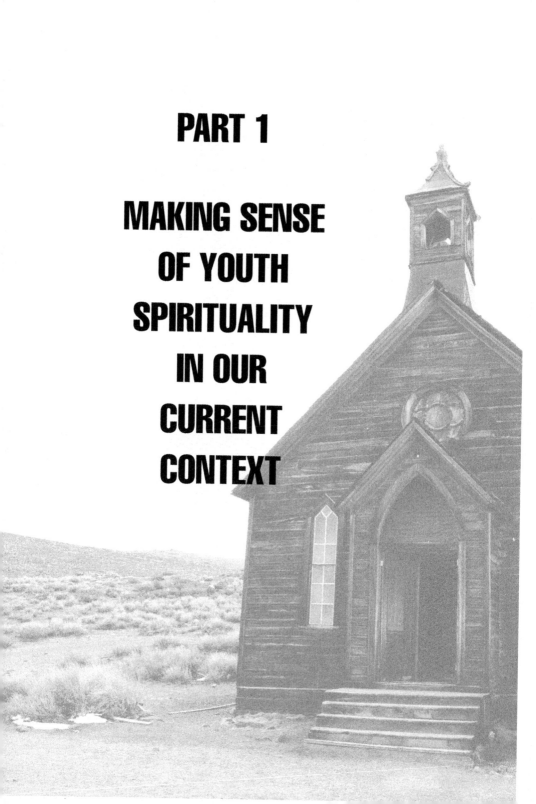

PART 1

MAKING SENSE OF YOUTH SPIRITUALITY IN OUR CURRENT CONTEXT

THE MYTH OF NICE: WHY MAYBERRY IS NOT THE KINGDOM OF GOD

Just after the 1960s, a school of thought began to develop in our country's subconscious. We began to look back to the days of the 1940s and 1950s as a time and place where things were good and wholesome. As we remembered our country's history, we developed the myth of Mayberry. The myth of Mayberry goes something like this: There is an order and reason to why everything happens. If you work hard and are honest, you will be successful, well-liked, and stable. Those who do bad things will reap the reward of their dishonesty and deception. The Mayberry myth holds kindness, honesty, and manners as signature virtues. In Mayberry, we look alike and talk alike, we smile and wave as we walk by, and everyone has a place. All problems are realized, solved, and reconciled in a 30-minute time frame and usually with an agreed-upon moral lesson to cap it all off. In Mayberry, there is order, happiness, values, and a sense that everything is going to be OK; even Otis, the town drunk, puts himself in the tank to sober up after one too many swigs from the bottle. As Americans, we believe that this time actually existed; and so many of us strive to reclaim this way of life. We find ourselves doing so by perpetuating the same moralistic dogmas of Mayberry, believing that living by these platitudes and niceties, we can somehow achieve a Mayberry-esque kingdom of God.

We are not called to have simple solutions to simple problems.

We are not called to live clean, neat, and tidy lives.

We are not called to be nice.

We are called to something so much more.

Nice is, well, nice. There is nothing wrong with being nice. We could use some more nice in our world. I realize this every time I drive in heavy traffic. Nice is taking turns letting people in from an on ramp; nice is picking up something that someone dropped; nice is opening a door for a stranger; nice provides excellent, tear-jerking footage for those insurance commercials, where we "pay it forward." I like nice. We have a great lack of nice in our world. When we witness it, we are often inspired to be nice.

Mayberry is nice.

Walking into a place where "everybody knows your name" is nice.

Nice makes us feel good.

Yea for nice!

Nice youth ministries strive to keep kids away from "the three Ds" of youth ministry: *drinking, drugs,* and *doing It.* Nice youth ministries work diligently to make sure that youth are having a great time, providing wholesome, fun activities, retreats, and Bible studies that will produce good kids who do good things, go to church and will ultimately repopulate the pews with their nice families. This does not work.

Here is what we know:

> Youth are losing interest in church.[1]

> They are leaving church.[2]

> They are not coming back.[3]

"If we don't reach this generation, it won't be because we didn't entertain them, but because we didn't dare them to take Jesus seriously"—**Shane Claiborne**

The 'Y' Myth

I grew up going to my local YMCA. It was the place where I spent my summers. I swam, played tennis and basketball, played dominos with the old timers, worked out, and learned how to flirt. The "Y" was a place that provided good, wholesome, fun and entertainment. I was never bored, always wanted to go, and always felt at home at the "Y." Some of our student ministries, head pastors, and parents would give anything for results half as good as the "Y" experienced. Not only have we wanted those results, we have employed many of the same techniques. We provide gyms, vending machines, rec leagues, and game rooms. We do whole summers dedicated to fun, games, and "reach" events. We have worked so diligently to provide an entertaining, safe, welcoming place where youth can have fun that we've lost our identity and, in turn, lost our soul.

We began to look more like organizations and companies instead of movements and entities of change. We traded in third-hand couches for leather couches, simple retreats for expensive youth trips, and an old basketball hoop for multi-million-dollar "Family Life Centers."

19

We did this with the best intentions—to "reach the teenagers"—and in doing so, entered into the deadly, never-ending entertainment wars. When we model ourselves after TV, concerts, and movies, we are putting ourselves into a competition against entities to which we will lose every time. We will lose because we are playing their game, on their turf, by their rules. We will lose because it is not in the church's DNA to be places of entertainment. If you've ever doubted this, take five minutes and look at almost any popular Christian programming. It's generally a poorly attempted knock-off of some wildly popular piece of media created for the purpose of entertaining.

> *Can youth group be fun?* Yes.
> *Should youth group be fun?* Yes.
> *Should fun be an objective of youth group?* No.

Unfortunately, there are still so many youth ministries that believe in order to be relevant they have to be like the "Y." What I believe we are beginning to understand is that the "Y" is better at being the "Y" than we are, and the entertainment industry is better at entertaining than we are. Somewhere along the way, we became convinced that the message of Jesus we were preaching was not appealing, scandalous, life-changing, or counter-cultural enough.

> We were right.
> It wasn't.

The problem came when chose to not reexamine the message we were preaching about Jesus and chose to change the method by which we conveyed the message.

We've tried everything we know of to make the message we are delivering more appealing, palatable, entertaining, and attractive. Many of our techniques have worked: We get them in the door, excite them, and even entertain them. But at the end of the day, the majority don't come back, will not stay, and will live lives that look very similar to their friends who never walk through the doors of a church.

What if we've focused on changing the wrong thing?

What if it had very little to do with the packaging?

What if the core of our problem was not our delivery but the message we were delivering?

What if our youth are opening beautiful, brightly colored packages that promise them their greatest desires, and they find nothing?

What if, in our best efforts to attract students, we dumbed down and diluted the very message and life that was attracting and keeping them in the first place?

L. Gregory Jones, a senior strategist for leadership education at Duke University said in a 2015 CNN interview, "Many young Christians seem bored with church." He notes that youth ministers have been ineffective at engaging students intellectual interests. He goes on to say, "Christianity in the United States hasn't done a good job of engaging serious Christian reflection with young people, in ways that would be relevant to their lives."[4] What if our students are not wanting more flash and glamour but are really desiring a deeper connection to their faith, ways to engage their most difficult questions, and a community in which to do that?

"These are kids who are dying for something worth dying for. There's only so much bubble gum and pizza they can take. Kids have been telling us for 25 years: enough already with the icebreakers. Give us something worth dying for. Then I'll come. The under expectation of teenagers is rampant in the culture and even more rampant in church—the very place that is supposed to call them to something worth dying for. How ironic."[5]
—**Kenda Creasy Dean**

The Adolescence Myth

Imagine taking one of your youth, placing him in the jungle by himself and telling him to hunt the goliath tarantula, the world's largest spider, with only some twine and a stick. Imagine telling the parents of a nine-year-old that their little girl will be responsible for taking her five-year-old brother to school, and along the way she will have to cross a raging river—in a hanging basket. Think about trusting your entire year's grain supply to the defense and security techniques of one of your junior high guys against 40 to 60 baboons with two-inch long fangs. For hundreds of thousands of people all around the world, these almost unimaginable scenarios are everyday realities. This stands in stark contrast to a culture like ours, whose helicopter parenting techniques rarely give youth the opportunities of responsibility, decision-making, and the consequences and rewards that follow.

In the majority of the world outside of Western culture, the idea of adolescence is virtually non-existent. We, in the American church, have downplayed the ability and thoughtfulness of adolescence. We have treated this notion of adolescent incompetence, as though it's mandated in the eleventh commandment: *Thou shalt be young, foolish and unable to process anything that is quasi-serious until you are 30.*

I'm not suggesting that the above examples are the standards by which we should understand our children's to-do lists, either. I do see a massive divide between their potential and actualized levels of growth and responsibilities.

We set our young people up to be lazy, irresponsible, and reckless. We do so through media, lack of responsibility, and parenting styles, beginning at a very young age. We tell youth, in no uncertain terms, that they cannot handle responsibility and are expected to fall short. In *Teen 2.0: Saving Our Children and Families From the Torment of Adolescence,* Robert Epstein argues that youth are not only capable of accepting large amounts of responsibility, difficult thought, and decision-making, they long for it. Through isolation, infantilization, and peer impact,[6] teenagers seem unintelligent and incapable; when these things are taken away and teenagers spend more time with adults, we see a dramatic shift in realized teenage potential.

Youth are longing for something more.

Harry, Frodo, and Katniss

We have seen this desire for responsibility from youth in the past fifteen years played out in popular young adult literature. In a time where teenagers are inundated with overprotective adults and institutions, it's no wonder they find an escape in places like Hogwarts, Middle Earth, and District 12. Characters like Harry, Ron, and Hermione from *Harry Potter*; Frodo and Samwise from *Lord of the Rings*; and Katniss and Peeta from *The Hunger Games* trilogy are recognizable by almost any youth in our country. While these stories are well written and entertaining, they hit a nerve much deeper and more central in our youth than the desire for a good read or an action-packed movie.

These characters are the embodiment of personal responsibility, the best possible risk-taking, and examples of someone rising above challenging situations on his or her own. Notice that in all three of these series, the characters are not subject to Epstein's isolation, infantilization, or impact of peers. From young ages, these characters have been in communities with a strong adult presence, from early ages they were in situations where they had to fend for themselves, and their closest peers were in similar situations. Youth have latched on to these books because these stories express their inner longing to make a difference in our world. These characters have given our youth the license to function in high capacities, in dangerous situations, and with complex problems. They have liberated our youth from the traps of modern parenting, limitations on youth culture, and even the narrow approach of the modern youth group. These characters are the realization of the inner longings and genetic formation of teenagers across America.

Do we empower the "Harrys" to fight darkness and injustice?

Do we encourage our young "Frodos" to journey toward their future?

Are we empowering and equipping the "Katnisses" to challenge and change the very core of our society?

If not, then we are missing the point.

Recent research has shown that teenagers are actually more competent than most adults.[7] This statement suggests major indictments for how we have done youth ministry for the past thirty years. We can no longer understand youth ministry as a training ground for raising adults who will numbly occupy pew space. We must realize that the most vibrant and potentially world-changing part of the church has, for the past thirty years, been relegated to the back rows and basements, when they should have been helping lead all of us into the future of the church.

After that I will pour out my spirit upon everyone;
your sons and your daughters will prophesy,
your old men will dream dreams,
and your young men will see visions. (Joel 2:28)

The Problem With Moralism: It's Just Not Christian

"Religion helps me not to do a lot of bad things"

"I guess it keeps me on the right track"

"It makes me a better person; you don't just go out and do immoral things"[8]

"God wants people to be good, nice, and fair to each other, as taught in the Bible and by most world religions."[9]

—Quotations from American teenagers about religion, in Christian Smith's *Soul Searching*

In Christian Smith's book *Soul Searching: The Religious and Spiritual Lives of American Teenagers,* the teenagers Smith interviews use these words to describe the goal of Christianity:

Nice

Kind

Pleasant

Respectful

Responsible

Self-improving

Taking care of one's health

Doing one's best to be successful[10]

This is the problem of moralism, the first member of the unholy trinity of the American teenage cultural religion. This religion has no challenges, no depth, no soul. This religion does not reflect the teaching of Jesus. You cannot practice this religion and stand against injustice, sacrifice oneself, and lose everything in the name of Christ. The tenets of this religion call one to avoid conflict, not to be a peacemaker within it.

We are not wired to practice this religion. We and our youth are wired to strive toward active holiness, not the sedentary faith of moralism.

Some Ways to Fight off Moralism

I believe that there are some important dichotomies that have to be drawn and distinguished between when we discuss moralism. I'm not usually a huge fan of drawing dichotomies. The technique, however, can be very useful when two ideas stemming from different sources have merged into one. When this happens, we usually lose the ability to distinguish between the two. This is what has happened in the case of moralism. Two ideas, American moralistic values and the identity of the believer propagated by Jesus, have been melded together in an almost indistinguishable form. It is time to pull them apart.

Is It American, or Is It Christian?

Early in my ministry, I had an experience with a parent that really confused me. Her son was in our senior high ministry. He was consistently going against the leadership, lying, and participating in very questionable practices. I had talked to his mother several times about these problems, with little to no support. I was in the church hallway with this mother, her son, and another young man the same age. The young man burped (to his credit it was no subtle burp; it was a rafter shaker). The mother looked like someone had just kicked a puppy; and she began to chastise this kid: "I cannot believe you would do something like that! That is not Christian at all!" In a later conversation, she proceeded to tell me that we should require all of our youth to go to a local manners course, called Cotillion. Here, she said, our youth would learn what it means to conduct themselves in a good Christian manner. They would learn how to be polite, kind, and patriotic; use manners; and dance socially. Fortunately, I was able to redirect the conversation and flee before having to sign a contract for our youths' participation.

While this sort of interaction is extreme in some ways, at its core, it reflects a common misconception among churches and parents: To be a good Christian is to be a clean, safe, polite, model American. It makes Christianity into whatever the hosting nation or society deems culturally and socially appropriate.

> Christianity is not American.
> America is not Christian.

One of the first pieces we have to strip away from our youth ministries is the practice that equates the identity of our faith within the framework of cultural standards and norms. Our culture places a high value on politeness and patriotism. We try to overlay these societal norms and claim that they are explicitly Christian. It can be very difficult to separate our religion from our cultural norms. It requires our communities of faith to ask the difficult and sometimes unpopular questions of self and country. It requires us to follow in the ecclesial footsteps of our fathers and mothers in the faith. We can draw on the messages of Martin Luther King, Jr., going against the state because he answered to a higher power. And Martin Luther, seeing the corrupt marriage of church and state, put his life on the line not only to call it out but to lead a movement to change it. We need to look no further than our religion's namesake, knowing that part of the reason why Jesus hung on a Roman cross is because his message and actions overturned the social order and consequently made him a direct enemy of the state. Asking these difficult questions and making these sometimes divisive distinctions will ultimately help us come closer to the heart of the gospel and move farther away from kindness masquerading as religion.

Is It Political, or Is It Biblical?

Every time we allow a political party, movement, or leader co-opt the name Christian, we lose a piece of our identity and credibility in the minds of teenagers. The divisive religio-political climate of the past quarter century has not only caused youth to lose confidence in our political system, it has also caused many to reject religion on the basis that it is nothing more than a tool in the political agenda, or as Marx quoted, "Religion is the opiate of the masses."

I am in no way saying that our religion should be absent in the political arena. It is a part of who we are as citizens, so it has its proper place among the other things that influence our opinions and our voting trends. The problem comes when our party affiliations determine our religious convictions. Our youth see these actions and their inauthenticity radar goes off almost immediately. It is so

27

important for our youth to understand that our politics are defined by our religion—not the other way around. If special interest groups and political agendas define policy and opinions for people of faith, then our youth will have little to do with that faith. If, however, we appeal to the biblical text, the tradition of the ecclesial community, and ever-present voice of the divine calling us forward, our youth will not only be encouraged but will feel that they have a place and a voice.

By allowing our faith to shape our politics, our youth will also be liberated from a two-party solution and begin to think outside the accepted box. Author and speaker for the postmodern Christian faith Brian McLaren talks about this thinking as the third way. In doing this, we not only give our youth a more faithful way of understanding politics but we will also benefit the current political system and our world as a whole.

Homogenous Identity, or Being Our Authentically Created Selves?

Do you remember in the early '90s, when churches started to reach out to skater kids and grunge kids who listened to Nirvana? Remember when we built skate parks in the church parking lot and brought in "grunge Christian" bands? Youth ministries began to specialize their ministries to these "fringe" demographics. This was all fine and good until we began our Borg-like assimilation.

In case the Borg reference is lost on you, let me explain: I'm sort of a Trekkie. Not your typical "Shatner rules!" "Beam me up, Scotty!" kind of Trekkie. I am a TNG Trekkie. I fell in love with Jean Luc Picard and the whole crew of the USS Enterprise from *Star Trek: The Next Generation*.

Don't judge me.

In the later years of the show, a mechanical alien race began to threaten the crew and the entire universe. They flew around in a massive cube-shaped ship and assimilated beings from other cultures into their group. They outfitted these beings in a full mechanical suit and rewired their brains so that they did not have individual identities but looked, thought, and acted as one unit called The Borg.

Some of these fringe ministries looked a lot like the Borg plan of evangelism. We brought them in under the guise of keeping their distinguishable identifying qualities, that is, the skateboarder. Then we assimilated them into buying t-shirts with sayings like "Jesus was a Shredder" and forced them to listen to Nirvana songs re-written with terrible lyrics.

More recently, our homogenization tactics have trended away from skateboards and toward the Duggar family and *Duck Dynasty.* Other groups work the sorority and fraternity angle, while still others double down on the Christian subculture that rejects "the world" in exchange for its own exclusive language, t-shirts, celebrities and music.

We've tried to assimilate these unique individuals into our homogenous Borg-like existence. We look the same, talk the same, laugh at the same church jokes, and speak in the same Christian-ese. We even wear the exact same neon-green shirts while on a mission trip as we invade the closest Chick-fil-A® and devour all of its resources.

Very Borg-like.

We fail when we try to smooth out the rough edges; make them less weird; and make them look like the white-bread, cookie-cutter Christians who populate student ministries all across America. When we create this cultural expectation, we rob the youth and our churches of their God-created uniqueness. We eliminate the beautiful diversity of the Kingdom and exchange it for the comfort of a monotone faith.

We have a very real and needed opportunity to change the look, feel, and tone of our student ministries. We have the opportunity to transition our youth ministries from places where students learn religious platitudes and cultural niceties into places of radical acceptance, revolutionary love, deep questions, theological exploration, and liberating empowerment for our students. We have the opportunity to expose them to a God who values justice over being nice and who loves changing lives instead of maintaining the status quo.

We have the opportunity to invite youth into the radical way Jesus lived. We have the chance to walk with students out of the caves of cultural niceties and into the very real and gritty life of faith. We get to challenge students to take seriously the call of Christ in ways that are risky and unsettling and that create deep unyielding faith.

We have the ability to stop raising a bunch of bland, nice kids and start discipling a generation of young men and women whose faith trumps affiliations, norms, and culture.

The world is a beautifully troubling, complex place full of horror and wonder. Let's be the type of people who step into that world with our students, teaching them and experiencing together the goodness and grace of Christ's transforming power.

1. "Methodological Design and Procedures for the National Study of Youth and Religion (NSYR) Personal Interviews—Wave 2," page 14. *http://youthandreligion.nd.edu/assets/102494/w2_iv_guide.pdf.* (Accessed 14 September 2015.)

2. "Millenials Leaving the Church in Droves, Study Finds, by Daniel Burke. *http://www.cnn.com/2015/05/12/living/pew-religion-study*. (Accessed 14 September 2015.)

3. Pew Forum Study: "Religion Among the Millennials," by Allison Pond, Research Associate; Gregory Smith, Senior Researcher; and Scott Clement, Research Analyst, Pew Forum on Religion & Public Life. *http://pewforum.org/Age/Religion-Among-the-Millennials.aspx.* (Accessed 14 September 2015.)

4. L. Gregory Jones, in "Millenials Leaving."

5. Religious and Spiritual Practices of American Youth, Kenda Dean, page 8. *http://youthandreligion. nd.edu/assets/102567/youth_ministry_practitioners_on_religious_and_spiritual_practices_of_american_youth.pdf.* (Accessed 14 September 2015.)

6. *Teen 2.0 Saving Our Children and Families From the Torment of Adolescence*, by Robert Epstein, page 174.

7. *Teen 2.0*, Epstein, page156.

8. *Soul Searching*, Smith, page 151.

9. *Soul Searching* Smith, page 162.

10. *Soul Searching* Smith, page 163.

THE 12-STEP GOSPEL

THE PROBLEM OF RELIGION AS DIVINE THERAPY

"Moralistic Therapeutic Deism exists, with God's aid, to help people succeed in life, to make them feel good, and to help them get along with others – who otherwise are different—in school, at work, on the team, and in other routine areas of life."[1]—**Christian Smith on why MTD is so prevalent in our religious landscape,** *Soul Searching*

Twenty or thirty years ago, a common complaint began to resound in churches and youth groups all across America. These complaints came from congregants wanting the Bible to be more exciting and more relevant to their day-to-day lives. A certain group of innovative pastors such as Rick Warren and Bill Hybels heard this call and answered it by creating worship services and sermons that were engaging and spoke to the everyday needs of the people in their congregations. They crafted messages that answered the questions of parenting, friendships, and self-fulfillment. They bridged the gap between the ancient Hebrew text and twenty-first-century suburbia with clever graphics, easy to follow outlines, and catchy titles. Thus was born the twenty-first-century mega church, the self-help sermon, and the unintended start of the practice of religion as divine therapy. As mega churches grew, so did the desire of pastors, deacons, church councils, and vestries to become more "mega." In turn, our leaders began to read more and more church growth books by "mega" pastors. In doing so, they adopted many good structures and systems for growth but also adopted much of the understanding of religion as divine therapy. That model and variations of it continue to be the foundations for hundreds of mega churches all over the country.

I think that Rick Warren and Bill Hybels have contributed many good ideas and innovative thought in the understanding of the sermon and worship. However, one of the unintended results of this new ecclesial method was that people began to understand and practice Christianity that had a distinctive "seeker" orientation. "Seeker sensitive" became quite the buzz term among church planters and practitioners in the 1990s and through the turn the of the century. Churches across the country, evangelical and mainline, began to remove religious symbols, language, and art that could turn off or push away visitors (primarily baby boomers) who had been burned by the church. They provided comfortable theater-style seating, music that was soothing and pleasant, and an overall atmosphere of relaxation and peace. In this comfortable setting, they preached sermons that helped people process through their religious baggage; held classes that helped them do financial planning; and offered support groups to help them raise healthier, happier families.

Church began to look a lot less like church and more like theaters.

Sermons began to sound a lot less like sermons and more like therapy.

Christianity began to look a lot less like a movement and more like a Club Med for nice people.

THE RISE OF THE SELF HELP GOSPEL

"Where once the self was to be surrendered, denied, sacrificed, and died to, now the self is to be esteemed, actualized, affirmed, and unfettered." [2]
—James L. Nolan, *The Therapeutic State*

The move toward a more therapeutic lifestyle was in no way isolated to Christianity but was embraced by the culture at large. In 2008, the self-help industry generated more than $11 billion dollars,[3] and the market continues to grow. Not only have self-help books dominated the bestseller lists, but the onslaught of daytime self-help talk shows and radio programs have conditioned our collective conscience. Icons such as Dr. Phil have built entire empires on giving people ways to help themselves through emotional and psychological problems. We have become a culture preoccupied with self-help.

If you think that the number of best-selling secular, self-help books is impressive, go to your local Christian bookstore and watch that number rise dramatically.

In an effort to be both relevant and helpful, the church attempted to provide self-help from a Christian perspective; but no one had define a uniquely Christian way to understand self. Instead, the church co-opted and mirrored the larger cultural movement that placed self-actualization and fulfillment at the pinnacle. A loose form of modern social science and theory took precedent in every arena, from preaching to pastoral care to church architecture. Consequently, the gospel characterized by self-sacrifice, deprivation, and care for others slowly refocused on knowing yourself better and finding deeper happiness and joy in God.

It is important to pause here and recognize the importance of social psychology, advancements in understanding inner personal dynamics, and a deeper knowledge of the complex layers of the mind and self. The church is and should be deeply indebted to the discoveries and advancements from these fields. In its best forms, the information gained from these disciplines should constantly inform and shape how we understand and practice ministry. Unfortunately, much of the Christian populous has latched on to the pop culture versions of this field; and consequently, our theological and ecclesial practices have suffered. Many of our youth have grown up in churches where the majority of the sermons they have heard rests somewhere between a 12-step program and a pep rally for Jesus. It's no wonder that the product of this sort of spiritual nourishment has such a construed view of Jesus and religion.

MY JESUS IN A BOTTLE

"When you are tempted to get discouraged, remind yourself that according to God's word, your future is getting brighter; you are on your way to a new level of glory. You may think you've got a long way to go, but you need to look back at how far you've already come. You may not be everything you want to be but at least you can thank God that you're not what you used to be."[4]

"Don't simply settle for what your parents had. You can go further than that. You can do more, have more, be more."[5]—Joel Osteen, *Your Best Life Now: 7 Steps to Living at Your Full Potential*

In 2006, Joel Osteen, pastor of Lakewood Church in Houston, was named by ABC News as one of the "10 Most Fascinating People of 2006," and "Most Influential Christian in America" by The Church Report. His book *Your Best Life Now*'s first printing sold more than 5 million copies and stayed on the New York Times Bestseller list for the majority of 2006 and 2007. Osteen has more than 40,000 people attending five services weekly and a television audience of more than 7 million, making Lakewood the largest church in America. This does not include the more than 100 countries that broadcast his Lakewood Church's services.

In his books, Osteen boasts of getting out of speeding tickets, getting into first class, and nabbing the best parking spots—all because he is in God's favor. Now remember, this is not someone who preaches from a box at the corner of Delusion and Crazy Street. This is a man whose every preached word reaches the ears of millions of people.

And it's not just Pastor Osteen. You've heard the stories.

"I was having the most terrible day, I was looking for a parking spot at Walmart; and out of nowhere, one at the front of the parking lot opened up and I knew that God was looking out for me."

"We were down on our luck, the bills were overdue, and the collectors were coming. I prayed that God would take care of our situation; and the next day, there was a check in the mail for the exact amount we needed."

Is this how God works?

I love the movie *Disney's Aladdin*. What great characters—Aladdin, Jasmine, Abu. And who can forget the Genie, with just a little rub on the lamp and a wish and poof! Do you see where I'm going? What happens when one of our primary interactions with God and Jesus consists of recognizing a perceived need, praying, and poof! God shows up and grants the wish, and we sing the praises of our magic genie. Certainly, it's not always that simple; but the practical implications generally are. It is not always to the extreme of a Joel Osteen. The message generally goes like this: If we just believe enough, pray enough, and put ourselves in God's favor, we get the things we need.

This makes sense in most people's minds. And why not? God loves us; wants us to be happy; and in turn, wants us to have what we need. We see biblical examples of God providing for God's people in times of need. It doesn't hurt when a charismatic, good-looking guy with millions of followers tells you that it has worked for him and that it can work for you.

Here is the problem:

A starving five-year-old boy is sitting in filth in the earthquake ravaged slums of Port au Prince, Haiti.

An HIV/AIDS baby in the Sub-Saharan region of Africa has a body that is ravaged by a disease she had no part in contracting.

A family is trying desperately to conceive a baby to love and to hold, but another miscarriage destroys their hope.

A 13-year-old girl in Thailand has had her body sold again and again for the past three years by a group of men who have enslaved her in the sex trade.

A marriage of 20 years ends with the simple words, "I don't feel like I know you anymore."

A text cannot wait, he misses the stop sign, and a community mourns the loss of one of its children.

All of a sudden a God who gives me a parking place at Walmart or pays my cable bill and yet seems to not be able to hear the cries of the least of these is not a God I want to claim.

Aladdin's genie becomes a much less exciting way of understanding our God.

THE GOSPEL IS NOT MY LIFE COACH

"If you don't live a godly life, you will always think negative things."

"It [religion] makes you feel better."

"I'm bettering myself by doing it. I become a better person, more mature and responsible in my life."

"If I need something, I can just pray." [6]

"The central goal in life is to be happy and to feel good about oneself." [7]

—Quotations from American teenagers about therapeutic religion, in Christian Smith's *Soul Searching*

Along with the idea that Jesus functions in varying degrees as our genie in a bottle, another problematic tendency emerges. Building on the trend established in the previous section, we have not only understood God as someone who comes and meets our wants and desires in a genie-like fashion. God also helps us reach our fullest potential. God helps us feel happy and satisfied with ourselves and aids us in finding personal fulfillment. God becomes our life coach and the gospel becomes our 12-step manual for health, healing, and wholeness.

This trend is evident in many Christian bookstores. Placards, coasters, note cards, wind chimes, and even breath mints line the shelves, each with inspirational Bible verses that encourage us and promise a better tomorrow. As is the case with most retail stores, Christian bookstores offer a supply for this growing demand.

When we and our self-improvement are at the center of the gospel, the gospel will continue to look like a self-help manual.

Christian Smith observed in the National Study of Youth and Religion some shocking and problematic trends in youth's understanding of the focus of their faith and religion. As a part of the study, the interviewers would track the frequency of the words used to describe the youth's religious priorities and faith. These language trends were extremely telling about the focus of the religion of teenage America. The number of interviewees who mentioned theological concepts was all in the single digits except for the terms "personal sin" (47), "obeying God" (13), and "repentance" (12). Theological concepts such as the "kingdom of God" (5), "sabbath" (5), and "Trinity" (4) received minimal recognition, whereas "self-discipline," "social justice," and "justification" did not get a single mention from the 267 interviewees.

While the mentions of theological concepts were minimal, at best, the tracking of therapeutic mentions paints an entirely different picture. Topping the list, with 112 total mentions, were "personal feeling," "being," "getting or being made happy." "Feeling good about oneself and life" (99) and "feeling better about oneself and life" (92) came in a close second and third. It is important to note that these were two and three times more than the first most mentioned theological and eight to ten times more than the second most mentioned theological concept. Smith reports that the specific phrase "feel happy" was used more than 2,000 times.[8]

This portion of the study alone has massive theological implications not only about the focus of our youth's spirituality but also the apparent lack of knowledge of theological terms and concepts. While there is an obvious failure in terms of theological education, what is more disturbing is that the apparent practical function and meaning of religion has developed into little more than a life supplement added to placate and sustain our self-confidence and happiness. This is detrimental to our souls and the very soul of the faith we practice.

Are we satisfied with a religion whose purpose is to make us happy?

Is it any wonder our youth seem disinterested and disengaged?

Can we imagine a faith that had less to do with personal happiness and everything to do with joining the mission of God?

I think we can, and I know we should.

SOME WAYS TO FIGHT OFF THERAPEUTIC RELIGION

As we begin to refocus and relearn our role in creation and with God, we need to reorient our focus and adopt some new ways of being. I believe that most of us will experience an almost immediate withdrawal pain when we begin to wean off therapeutic religion. But it is not just about shifting the focus; it is also about finding our identities in the new light of our refocused theology.

Refocus on God's Reconciliation of All of Creation

In a time and culture that finds itself so consumed with personal self-improvement, it can be very easy to forget that we, as people of faith, follow a God who is in the constant process of reconciling all of creation. From the beginning of Scripture, God has been in the practice of drawing all of creation into a closer relationship with God's self. Along the way, our Western collective Christian conscience, probably with Augustine's help,[9] understood God's reconciliation as an intensely personal and individually focused work. Scripture attests to only personal reconciliation in its relation to the greater reconciliation of creation: Moses to lead the children, Jacob for Israel, Zacchaeus for the people he wronged, Saul for the gentiles. Again and again, the Scriptures demonstrate individual reconciliation in relation to God working for the greater love of all creation. God does love us as individuals but loves us and the rest of creation too much to let our individual reconciliation be God's primary focus or ours.

Respond to Jesus' Call to be Co-Laborers With God in This Reconciliation

After our youth begin to understand that God is not concerned with only their personal reconciliation, we then have the amazing opportunity to share that the biblical account is full of stories about how God has called God's people throughout history into being co-laborers in this work of reconciliation. God does not let us sit idly by while God works to bring creation closer. We have the opportunity and privilege to work alongside God. We get to be creative, innovative, and faithful as we work to realize the original intent of all things created. This is something not only to which youth can subscribe, but in which they will find a real and meaningful place. When we understand reconciliation as something that occurs far beyond the proximity of the individual, we then give youth and adults alike a mission; a common purpose; and ultimately, the ability to join with God, minister with the great physician, and create with the Creator.

Reclaim the Embodiment of the Suffering Christ

We as modern Americans are generally very uncomfortable around suffering. We are especially uncomfortable when suffering is very real and present in our lives or the lives of those close to us. As a society, we spend billions of dollars to deter the effects of aging, pain, and discomfort. We insulate ourselves and our families from as many forms of discomfort as possible. In a culture focused on self-improvement and hell-bent on realizing "Your Best Life Now," there is very little room for suffering and for those who suffer.

It has not always been this way.

In 1503, Matthias Grunewald was commissioned by an Antonine monastery in Isenheim, Germany, to paint a series of murals depicting Christ's suffering on the cross. The monastery's cloistered community understood its mission as a hospital for the sick and the dying.

In the central panel of the massive painting, Jesus is portrayed in the grotesque image of a diseased man covered with boils and sores, with a distended belly and webbed feet, hanging on a cross and writhing in pain.

Its purpose was to unite the patients' suffering with Christ so that they could embrace the process of dying with greater acceptance. In the hospital's healing program, patients were to be encouraged to meditate on the images while recognizing that Christ suffered with them so that they could embrace their suffering and possible deaths with peace.[10]

This monastery understood the gospel and calling of Christ not as something that shuns or flees from suffering but recognizes much of its mission and identity from within those liberating confines.

I often wonder whether we would recognize this Jesus.

> Jesus was not always sitting and smiling, surrounded by children and flowers.
>
> Jesus held lepers.
>
> Jesus comforted prostitutes.
>
> Jesus was beaten.
>
> Jesus died.

Our God is not a god who shies away from suffering. Throughout Scripture, God enters into people's suffering and embodies that suffering—even to the point of dying on a cross. We are called by Jesus himself to embrace suffering and pain.

> Carry your cross.
>
> Turn the other cheek.
>
> Love your enemy.
>
> Pray for your persecutors.
>
> Blessed are you when others hurt you.

The followers of Jesus have been no strangers to pain and suffering. Throughout history, people have been beaten, tortured, and killed for their faith. People have not just suffered and joined alongside the suffering; they have also been comforted and inspired by the suffering of Jesus.

There are massive amounts of suffering in our world and in the lives of our youth and their families. To "claim" the version of the gospel that says that Jesus is going to bless us, fix our problems, and get us out of speeding tickets in the midst of that suffering cheapens the gospel and creates a division between those who suffer and those who do not. One of the greatest gifts we can give our youth is the ability to embrace suffering and those who suffer.

These practices of sacrifice and the (re)discovery of our role in these practices not only subverts the overwhelmingly therapeutic nature of our modern Christianity, it makes it obsolete. When we move away from its self-absorption and into its self-sacrificing nature, we help heal and give therapy to others and, in turn, mend our own hearts.

1. *Soul Searching,* Smith, page 169.
2. *The Therapeutic State: Justifying Government at Century's End,* by James L. Nolan, page 3.
3. PRWeb's "Self-Improvement Market in U.S. Worth $9.6 Billion" *http://www.prweb.com/releases/Marketdata/Enterprises/prweb440011.htm.* (Accessed 14 September 2015.)
4. *Your Best Life Now: 7 Steps to Living at Your Full Potential,* by Joel Osteen, page 65.
5. *Your Best Life Now,* Osteen, page 65.
6. *Soul Searching,* Smith, page152.
7. *Soul Searching,* Smith, page 163.
8. *Soul Searching,* Smith, page 167–168.
9. Augustine was quoted as saying, "God loves each of us as if there were only one of us" and a number of derivative quotations.
10. Andree Hayum, "The Meaning and Function of the Isenheim Altarpiece: The Hospital Context Revisited." *The Art Bulletin* 59 (1977): 501–17.

THE UNCONTAINABLE GOD

PANCAKES AND WAFFLES

"God does not need to be particularly involved in one's life except when God is needed to resolve a problem."[1]
—**An American teenager's response to God's presence and activity in everyday life, from Christian Smith's** *Soul Searching*

When I have my choice, my favorite meal to cook is, without a doubt, brunch. One of my favorite parts of brunch is having pancakes and waffles. Pancakes are great, but my true love is waffles. I love their crispy ridges, fluffy insides—and let's not forget their deep wells in which to pour fruit, syrup, or sometimes a little whipped cream. If the wells are small enough, I also like to make for my kids little designs such as smiley faces, their initials, or characters by pouring syrup into the little compartments on the top of the waffle. The compartments keep everything separate, or "compartmentalized," if you will. Compartments are great for waffles, diaper bags, and Batman's utility belt; however, they are not good for religion or spirituality.

When I talk to youth about spirituality, I usually use the pancake/waffle metaphor. I tell them that some people practice waffle faith, where they are able to compartmentalize the places that the syrup (your faith, belief, God) can go. They can control what parts of their life faith will be a part of; how much; and more important, where it will not go. I tell youth that people will sometimes let faith go into their family compartments and their spirituality compartments. Often, they will not let their faith go into other compartments such as how they practice their business, how they talk about others, or how they handle bad drivers. The problem with waffle faith is that God isn't really into waffles. God's more of a pancake God.

I try to get my youth to grasp the idea that God does not like to be limited and compartmentalized. Don't believe me? Ask anyone from Jonah to Zacchaeus to Saul. The Christian God has never been one for affecting certain areas and leaving others alone. We see this most profoundly in the ministry of Jesus. First-century Judaism had a certain way of understanding God, what God did, and even whom God loved. According to that practice, God lived in one building, God was relegated to certain religious practices and customs, and whole groups of people were excluded by that way of understanding God. Prostitutes, tax collectors, and people with diseases were not, according to that time period, people whom God wanted and so were shunned, accordingly. There were a lot of God waffles being made. Then Jesus came along and showed us that God preferred pancakes to waffles.

God wants to inhabit, cover, and invade every part of our lives. From our most private to our most public parts, God wants to cover every square inch of who we are. Just like the pancake, God does not want or need containing. God wants to cover, saturate, and flavor every part of our being and our life.

THE COMPARTMENTALIZATION OF AMERICAN LIFE AND RELIGION

"Deism is the belief in a particular kind of God: one who exists, created the world, and defines our general moral order, but not one who is particularly personally involved in one's affairs—especially affairs in which one would prefer not to have God involved. . . . The God of this faith keeps a safe distance."[2]—**Christian Smith,** *Soul Searching,* **on deism**

The problem of compartmentalization is both personal and cultural. We, as modern Americans, are really good at compartmentalizing our lives. Some of this behavior is purely for survival purposes. We are taught from a very early age that we need to keep things separate: work and home, school and play, church and state.

Sometimes these dichotomies are natural; other times they are forced. Sometimes they make sense; other times they make us crazy. Sometimes they are good; other times they tear at our soul. I cannot tell you how many students whose lives and identities I see torn between these dichotomies. In one ear, a parent says how important church and faith are; but in the other ear, sports, school, and social status always takes precedent over church. Students are told that honesty and hard work are virtues; but as soon as the work becomes overwhelming or they are not able to study for the test, cheating and taking prescription drugs to get ahead become perfectly acceptable. Girls in my youth group are told that they are beautiful creations of God but are not asked to dances because "they need to lose a few pounds."

When we try to or are forced compartmentalize something as central to us as our faith, it forces us to live double- and triple-masked lives.

We also frequently compartmentalize our issue-based thinking. Whether right or left of the aisle, we rarely allow our belief and religion to mix

45

with politics, science, and social issues. Not only are our issues and social roles compartmentalized but so are moral constructs and reasoning.

I don't mean that all compartmentalizations are bad. I don't want my senior high football players to come to youth group and begin tackling our freshly arrived seventh grade students. The compartmentalization is detrimental when it is applied to the places where we choose to allow God and the gospel to be present and the places where we do not allow their presence.

> *"Moral decision making in therapeutic individualism is always profoundly individually self-referencing. Right and wrong are determined not by external moralities derived from religious teachings, natural law, cultural traditions, or the requisites of collective social functioning."*[3]

I remember having a conversation with Mark, a student who'd just had one of those "aha" moments. We were serving at a homeless shelter, and Mark met a homeless man who blew away all of Mark's preconceived notions of why homeless people are homeless. Through their conversation, Mark found out that the man was once a computer programmer, with a great house, a wife, and two kids. He lost his job and made a few self-acknowledged bad decisions; his wife and kids moved out; and before he knew it, he found himself among America's homeless population. The man's revelation shocked Mark. It stunned him that most Americans are only one or two paychecks away from homelessness. Mark had grown up in a family where he was taught that people were homeless because they were lazy, alcoholics, or drug addicts. Instead of letting this revelation, an experienced truth, inform and change his paradigm, he understood this homeless man's story as the exception and continued his perception that homeless men and women are drunks, drug addicts, and bums and that because of this behavior, they do not deserve help. It was so interesting and distressing to see how Mark was able to compartmentalize what he believed to be true, from his real-life experience.

I continue to be amazed at how many people will consistently argue against things that Jesus said about the poor, the outcast, and the dejected. They don't argue that Jesus' teachings are outdated or should be interpreted differently. The arguments generally go along the lines of "that will not work" or "that is just not what I believe." I've even had others tell me that "Jesus had a naive understanding of the world." When I probe their statements, I find people's views are generally informed more by the political party they affiliate with, their annual income, or their place in society.

Smith says, "Therapeutic individualism is not so much a consciously and intentionally held ideology, but rather a taken-for-granted set of assumptions and commitments about the human self, society, and life's purpose that powerfully defines everyday moral and relational codes and boundaries in the contemporary United States." [4]

So much of American religion, and consequently youth ministry in America, finds its foundations in a subconscious ideology based upon our *Sitz im Leben*,[5] a German phrase meaning "place in life" or "life situation." When I push youth on their responses to social issues, I get vague answers, at best; and they typically respond with, "Well, that is just how it is" or "that is what I believe." These statements support the American compartmentalization of faith and religion. We even go to great apologetic lengths to make compartmentalization work and still maintain that we make faith-based decisions. This is modern deism at its best.

DON'T SAY THAT IN CHURCH!

You're walking down the hall after youth group. Several junior high guys are standing in a corner mumbling; and all of a sudden, an eruption of laughter comes from the guys. The majority of the group is pointing to one of the other guys; and without fail, someone blurts out, "Dude! You can't say that in church!"

When I hear my kids say this sort of thing, the first thing I ask them is, why? Why do you not feel comfortable saying something in this building but apparently feel comfortable saying it on the street outside the church? Generally, the answers are something like:

> *"Well, it's God's house."*
>
> *"It is disrespectful."*
>
> *"I am afraid lightening might strike me."* (We are inside, by the way.)
>
> *"Because this is church, and God lives here."*

I remember growing up not only saying some of those same things but also having them reinforced by adults in the church. We were taught that we had to act a different way inside the walls of the church. It was ingrained in us that inside those walls, we had to have a different respect for God. That's a great crowd control method for rambunctious junior high guys, but I think that it is pretty harmful theology for youth and the rest of the faithful.

I get it. It's helpful. It's even biblical in some ways. We see the Temple being a very sacred place in both the Hebrew Bible and the New Testament. But Scripture is also very clear about God's omnipresence. God is everywhere, not to be confined, concealed, or restricted. Similarly, we are to worship and respect God everywhere. When we place precedent on certain times and places to interact with and worship God, we are compartmentalizing God yet again. Our students pick up on this and will mirror this attitude.

It is incredible how the church, unknowingly, has indoctrinated so many people with the understanding that God has a cot and a pillow just above the choir loft.

ESCAPE POD THEOLOGY

In the previous chapter, we established that I am a TNG junkie. In case you skipped the last chapter (shame on you), TNG is *Star Trek: The Next Generation*. In TNG as well as with any other spaceship, submarine, James Bond-esque film or television show, sometimes there is a need for an escape hatch. A little—usually egg-shaped—one- or two-person escape pod. The escape pod becomes important when things get a little too rough or the ship explodes and someone has to make a quick escape. The escape hatch is a clever mechanism that gets a number of good (and sometimes bad) guys out of a sticky situation.

Sometimes the message of the church has been that we should adopt an escape pod mentality.

Escape pod theology teaches that this world is bad or evil; that our bodies are bad or evil; that all of creation is in an unstoppable perpetual downward spiral into the deep, dark abyss of eternity; and your seat belt is stuck. We're often trapped in a dualistic understanding of world and self, where the only good things are the ones to come or are beyond this current time and place. This theology always puts God in the future in that time and place, with us desperately trying to get to the escape pod before the ship goes down.

That is not the God or the creation represented in the Scripture.

Throughout the Hebrew Bible and New Testament, we see escape pod theology refuted, from the beginning of Creation to a God who walks, talks, and lives in the middle of this creation. Throughout Scripture, we see holy places being recognized, not just in some dream of a far off place, but in the middle of the Jordanian desert and the walls of Jerusalem. Throughout history, people have marked these "thin places." These markers have been everything from a pile of stacked stones to grand cathedrals built in the most lavish baroque styles. It is not that God is somehow more present in these places but that these are special placeholders to recognize where people have experienced the ever-present God in very special ways. Humanity has not only recognized God here among us but has been so affected by this presence that we have made it a point to mark it for others throughout history to be able to come and be blessed by it as well. God has invested a lot in creation, one proclaimed as "doomed" by escape pod theologians.

When we push against the sinking ship trend, we allow our youth to step away from the pod hatches and begin to see God right here and not somewhere far off. So much of our Christian culture's trend toward this modern form of deism is due in part to the church's rejection of the very place that God created.

We have allowed and even encouraged our youth to think, "If this place is so bad that we have to escape it ASAP to go and be with God, then logic tells me that there is no way in the world that God is here."

If we want our youth to believe that "God is here," then we first have to help them understand that "here" is not the seventh level of hell; it is actually the place that God made and where God wants to be with us. Right here. Right now.

SOME WAYS TO ADDRESS MODERN DEISM

There are some new and not-so-new modes of thinking and operating that we have to adopt in order to combat modern deism. I say that these are new and not-so-new because, while these ideologies are not in mainstream practice, they have been in practice for thousands of years, operating at the fringes of our faith. These three theological ideas develop a more holistic faith, where we discover that God is not only present but actively working everywhere, at every moment, and in everything. This not only contradicts a distant God, it denounces a god who is distant as being no god at all.

Every Thing Is Spiritual

I borrowed this title from Rob Bell. It is not mine. But it is good, and it is true.

I love to talk with my students about the holy thumbprint. I dabble in clay sculpting and throwing on a pottery wheel. I find these activities very therapeutic, in the most real and helpful way, and a great way to express things beyond the weight that words can carry. When I first started throwing pottery I wanted so badly for my vases, lamps, and bowls to like ones that I had seen in shops. My teacher, in her stern but kind way, told me that it was none of my business to try to make pieces that others had made. I was to make what I was to make and nothing else so that when I created something, it was mine, by me, and from a place inside me. The second thing I quickly learned was that I could never turn out a piece that did not have some mark that I had sculpted it. I could not escape those little "imperfections" on my pieces. Usually, these imperfections were highlighted by a fingerprint left on the clay before firing. My teacher let me in on a little secret that stuck with me. She said that a machine can make a "perfect vase." She said that those machine-made vases are sold by the thousands every day at a little shop down the road—Walmart. She then told me that what differentiated the $2.99 Walmart special and a $299 piece were those little things I called flaws. What I came to learn is that those imperfections are the marks of the sculptor, almost signatures, if you will. For me, those flaws often came in the form of a thumbprint.

God leaves thumbprints all over creation.

Whether it is a mountain, the setting sun, a child's laugh, the songs of a tribe in Uganda, or the faint breathing of an elderly man in the ICU, everything is spiritual. The thumbprints of our creator are all over the great masterpiece of creation.

To help draw our students and their families away from modern deism, we need to help them understand the deep spirituality of everything that they encounter, to hear a bird's song or sit through a traffic jam and understand that each has spiritual implications. When we understand that everything is spiritual, we have a much more difficult time disconnecting our actions, thoughts, desires, and choices from our spirituality. Eventually, we will understand all of those things not just as elements that need to be influenced by spirituality but that they in and of themselves are deeply spiritual.

Every Place Is Holy

When most people think of New Orleans, Louisiana, a few things pop into their heads: Cajun cooking, alligators, and the infamous Bourbon Street. New Orleans has won two distinct awards every year for as far back as most people can remember: The city with the best night life and America's dirtiest city.[6] New Orleans is a city known for "wild" videos, dirt, the largest rowdiest party in America. And it's known for Bourbon Street, certainly not a holy site.

One of the cool things about God is that God does not ask our opinion about where holy places can and cannot be.

New Orleans really is one of the most unlikely places to call holy; but for the 130 or so high school students and adults I take there every year, it is one of the most holy places on earth. For the past seven years, we have taken our senior high mission trip to New Orleans to continue the ongoing Hurricane Katrina rebuilding effort. We have been the first groups in the houses; and after six years, we have seen the devastation, we have heard the stories of heartache and loss, and we have seen our God along every step of the way. A place that is known for all sorts of "unholy" practices has become a massive altar for our group.

It was not always this way.

Before I tell you why, let me tell you about "site stories." Site stories are an element of our nightly worship on mission trips. I explain to the youth that God is everywhere. God is even on our worksites during the day. I tell them that sometimes we cannot see God or what God is doing because we do not have our "God goggles" on. I tell them that God goggles work when we change how we look at our world, work, and the people who are around us. When we begin to look for God at work, we usually see some pretty amazing God things happening all around us. We use our site story time as an element in worship where any youth or adult can come up and share how he or she or the group saw God that day. It really is my favorite part of worship.

Now back to the bad part.

Our first year in New Orleans we were introduced to what became our arch-nemesis, mold remediation. If you say those two words to any youth in my senior high group, he or she will give you an evil look just before running in the opposite direction. Each year, we rebuild Katrina houses with a local non-profit organization called The St. Bernard Project.[7] In The St. Bernard Project's process, mold remediation is the first step of work when moving a family back into their home. When these houses are left untouched for years, all sorts of terrible mold grows on the boards. A family cannot move in unless this mold is gone, so you have to have mold remediation. Here is the down and dirty of it: First you put on your respirator. (By the way, did I mention that it is hovering between 99 and 102 degrees, with a 115-degree heat index?) In some situations, you also put on your hazmat suit. Then you proceed to scrub every board in the house with a wire brush, reactivating the mold. Then you mark the board with an *X*. Next you soak paper towels in a foul chemical called Shockwave and then wipe down each surface of every board in the house to kill the reactivated mold, but you have to make sure it has an *X*. Then you put a circle around the *X*. Finally you then paint every board that has a circle and *X* with Kilz®. It's a rough process.

During site story time on our first trip, we heard story after story about the horrors of mold remediation. It was not fun work. It was too hot. I hate mold remediation! On the third night of hearing this in our site story time, one of our college students, named Phillip, got up to tell a site story. He talked about the mold remediation process in a pretty comical way. Then beyond the comedy and heartache of mold remediation, he said, "Isn't it amazing that's all it takes for a family to get to have a home again?"

Boom!

It was amazing: What felt like a 115-degree hell became a little piece of heaven on earth. It was the first stone laid of the altar that we have continued to build as a group in New Orleans. It is an altar that we return to every year in the dirtiest city in America.

Whether it is an amazing experience at camp or hanging out with friends or the 115-degree swamp heat of New Orleans, helping our youth understand that God is present in all of those places will certainly discourage and eliminate any idea that God is somewhere else.

How are we helping kids build altars wherever they go?

Every Moment Is Sacred

We mark our lives by certain moments in time. The question used to be, "Where were you when Kennedy was assassinated?" or "What were you doing when Pearl Harbor was attacked?" Now the question is typically, "Where were you on 9/11?" We also mark our lives by joyous events such as getting our driver's license, graduating from high school, getting married, or having children. We do the same thing with our spirituality. We mark our spiritual lives with milestones such as baptism, first Communion, accepting Jesus, confirmation, and entering youth group. While all of these are incredibly important and faith forming, they are few and far between. The times in between often feel somewhat like a "dead time." These times, like every moment we are taking in breath, are sacred moments. Some of the most compelling and sacred times in Scripture come in these seemingly uneventful pauses.

We in the church do a great disservice when we put such great emphasis on Sunday morning worship. In doing so, we unintentionally tell our youth, "Yes, we believe that God is always here in every moment; but for this hour, God is really, *really* here— like, way more than usual!" Instead of perpetuating this idea that God shows up according to our worship schedule or comes only to our "Wonderful Wednesday Night Wowapolooza," we should help students understand that God is everywhere. We need to help them understand that every moment is sacred because God is active and alive in each moment.

54

We run the risk of decentralizing our programming and influence. But shouldn't that be the point? Should we not want to decentralize what we are doing so that God, who is in every moment, in every situation, and in every thing, can be centralized? When we decentralize, we no longer get to decide when God is talking, other than to say that God is always talking. We no longer get to proclaim that God is here, except to say that God is always here.

The worst that can happen is we will begin to sound a lot more like Jesus and will see God in places we never thought God would be seen.

That sounds a little like the Gospel.

The Jailbreaking of God
Christ be with me, Christ within me,
Christ behind me, Christ before me,
Christ beside me, Christ to win me,
Christ to comfort and restore me.
Christ beneath me, Christ above me,
Christ in quiet, Christ in danger,
Christ in hearts of all that love me,
Christ in mouth of friend and stranger.
—The Breastplate Prayer of St. Patrick

What if we busted God out? What if we planned a daring escape for God? An escape would have to involve loads of people, time, and effort. We would have to have the help of experts and novices, of professionals and janitors. Some of the plan would have to be an inside job, but other folks would have to provide help once God was on the outside. Security is tight, even state-of-the-art, and has been almost impenetrable for thousands of years. But it can be done, and it has before.

I know that it probably is not that dramatic; but in all honesty, sometimes it feels that way. It feels like in order for our culture to be able to see God outside of the boxes and neat little compartments we have so handily put God in, we need a jailbreak.

We need to jailbreak God personally.

We need to jailbreak God culturally.

When God is constricted to our cultural constraints, preferences, and voting records, it becomes pretty difficult for God to be God. I think that God is tired of being locked up in the clink and is itching for some walking around time.

What do you think will happen when God is let free, to be here and there, just as God pleases? Can you imagine the amount of trouble God would cause in our world, in our country, and in our personal lives? It could be tragic.

Wouldn't that be amazing?

What would happen if we were to stop acting like waffles and began to practice pancake spirituality, letting God into every part of our thinking, actions, decisions, and lives? We need to jailbreak God. It is not for God's sake that this needs to be done, it is for ours. We, our youth, their parents, and grandparents all need God to be broken out of these constrictions of what we deem proper and prudent. What if we let God's goodness run through our choices and our lifestyles? What if we stop believing that God has God's place on Sunday morning and begin to understand that every time and every place is God's?

Thank God for that.

The jailbreak is on.

1. *Soul Searching*, Smith, page 155.
2. *Soul Searching*, Smith, page 165.
3. *Soul Searching*, Smith, page 173.
4. *Soul Searching*, Smith, page 172.
5. Term, roughly meaning "place in life," coined by German theologian Hermann Gunkel.
6. *Time* Magazine's "The Ten Dirtiest Cities in America: New Orleans Tops the List," by Alyson Krueger. *http://newsfeed.time.com/2011/06/14/the-ten-dirtiest-cities-in-america-new-orleans-tops-the-list.* (Accessed 15 September 2015.)
7. St. Bernard Project: *http://www.stbernardproject.org.* (Accessed 15 September 2015.)

MEISM: THE PROBLEM OF 140 CHARACTERS

"Someone has to tell teenagers that to study hard in order to get into the right school so you can land the right job so you can afford the right spouse so you can have the best 2.3 kids in a house with a white picket fence is not God's plan/ dream for our lives."—**Dr. Fred Edie, Associate Professor of the Practice of Christian Education; Director, Duke Youth Academy for Christian Formation**

It was the 2006 MTV Europe Music Awards. A European band named Justice had just won the Video of the Year award. They were accepting the award, when another musician arrived, uninvited, on the stage and grabbed the microphone. Kanye West began his now famous tirade: "Hey, if I don't win, the award show loses credibility. . . . It's nothing against you. I've never seen your video. It's nothing against you, but, heeell, no."[1] This in and of itself is shocking. It is difficult to imagine the audacity one person would have to have to hijack a moment set aside to celebrate another person and make it all about himself. What seemed almost worse were the reactions of the spectators caught on camera. They were laughing, clapping, and cheering Kanye on. A few years later, it happened again. This time it was in America, and the victim was Taylor Swift. We've all seen that one. And yet Kanye is still adored by millions of fans. In another instance, when he was on stage for an award that he actually won, Kanye said, after what seemed like a heartfelt statement about his grandmother, "My greatest achievement still is . . . I still think I am the greatest."

This narcissism is grotesque, disgusting, and all too common.

Dr. Nathan DeWall says in his paper to the American Psychological Association, *Tuning in to Psychological Change,* that narcissism is on a dramatic rise in pop music. This is generally the time to cue the onslaught of criticisms of culture and its effects on youth. But Dr. DeWall says that just the opposite is true. In an interview with NPR's Michelle Norris, DeWall states that music is a "mirror of cultural changes in personality, traits, and motivations and emotions."[2] His paper focuses on the increase in this sort of thought in music in the past 30 years, which reflects this line of thought in culture. We find it from Fergie belting out the ballad of her "lady lumps" to TuPac proclaiming to the world that "All Eyez on Me." If these songs are really an indicator of our love of self, then there is a fiery romance brewing every time we step in front of a mirror.

WHAT EXACTLY DOES PARIS HILTON DO?

"In the twentieth century, 'character' gave way to 'personality.'"

"The over-praised American personality expects regularly to assess the worth of others, regardless of his qualifications for doing so."[3]—**Christine Rosen, "The Overpraised American"**

It is interesting that one person's celebrity can be based on nothing else than being that person. Paris Hilton, for example is an heiress, she parties, and she was on a reality show whose plot line was little more than being an heiress and partying. Really, that's all Paris Hilton does; and she draws constant media frenzy everywhere she goes. I know that it would be easy to begin to slip down a utilitarian iced slope here, but she literally does nothing beyond show up somewhere and has pictures taken of her going through her normal everyday motions. This country pays her millions of dollars just to be Paris Hilton. She is not alone.

> We have celebratized the mundane, the ordinary, the truly un-interesting.

A few years back an up-and-coming new cruise line called Celebrity Cruises burst on the scene. It promised to treat everyone like a celebrity. Its slogan was even "Celebrity Cruises, Starring You." I understand that this is a brilliant marketing campaign, but isn't it interesting how that reflects our culture of meism? I want to be the star. I want to be the center of attention. All eyes on me.

We see meism transcend the world of advertising and filter into the brave new world of social media. When Facebook launched in 2004, I remember hearing the questions over and over, "What are we going to do with it?" and "Why would people care what my 'status' is; and by the way, what is a status anyway?"

> People caught on quickly.

When a résumé comes across my desk, I immediately skip over the references; and I go straight to Facebook, where the applicant is the star. I can find out everything about someone, what he likes, her favorite movies, his favorite books, and even her political views. I can see what his interactions are with his friends, whether we have any mutual friends. And I can find out (in pictorial detail) what she did on spring break 2008.

I also remember when Twitter became mainstream. Again, I would hear people ask things like, "What's a tweet?" "Are you my tweep?"

and "What does it mean to twit?" I also heard statements along the lines of, "Why in the world would I want to tell everyone what I am doing all of the time; and furthermore, why would I want to know what others are doing all of the time?"

Again, we've figured it out.

In the 2015 Pew Research Center study, "Teens, Social Media & Technology 2015," it is clear just how well we've figured it out.[4]

92% of teens go online daily.

25% go online "constantly."

75% of teenagers have access to smartphones (on which most of their social media life is lived).

71% are on Facebook.

52% on Instagram.

41% are on Snapchat.

Isn't it interesting how we have systematized, commercialized, and subjected ourselves to this strange self-induced voyeurism?

David R. Smith writes, "A recent trend has developed in our (largely) narcissistic culture, taking (and posting) a 'wealthie.' If you're wondering what 'wealthie' is, just think 'wealth + selfie' and you'll get a pretty good idea. A 'selfie' is a picture you take of yourself standing in front of the high school art club's winning entry; a 'wealthie' is a picture you take of yourself standing beside the Mona Lisa . . . wearing a Rolex."[5]

I could go on and on about how Facebook has made our lives the focal point of the universe, how Twitter brought our most mundane actions and thoughts to the center of the arena, and how YouTube allowed us to "Broadcast Yourself" to the entire world. They, however, are not the problem. Social networking is not the cause of our meism; it is, however, the commercialized and capitalistic offspring of our love affair with ourselves. It is the need to know and judge others and to be judged ourselves. It has become the currency of our highly connected globalized social economy. Our worth is determined by hits, followers, likes, and friends whose status as such never requires a spoken word.

EVERYONE GETS A TROPHY, AND WE ALL END UP LOSING

"We're seeing an epidemic of people who are having a hard time making the transition to work—kids who had too much success early in life and who've become accustomed to instant gratification."—**Dr. Mel Levine, pediatrics professor, University of North Carolina Medical School**

When I was 10 years old, I played Little League baseball; and I was a pretty good third baseman. I started every game the entire season. When the time came for the coaches to select their teams' All-Stars, I thought that I had a pretty good chance of making the All-Star team. I waited on that phone call all night. It never came.

The next day, I was disappointed but not angry—until I found out who had made the All-Star team in the third base position: He wasn't some great player from another team but the kid who played backup to me. When I told my parents about the decision, they reminded me that my coach was the backup player's uncle and that might have had something to do with the coach's decision.

That's where we left it. My parents did not write a letter, cause a big stink, or threaten to sue the parks and recreation department. They told me that sometimes life would not be fair. I was heartbroken, but I learned some valuable lessons. Maybe the coach's decision was unfair. Maybe the coach knew that the team needed some talents this guy had more than the talent that I brought to the team. The thing I learned most was that just because things did not go the way I wanted them to go, did not mean that my parents were going to swoop in and fix everything.

Unfortunately, this story plays out much differently now in towns all across the country. Every year, I hear countless stories from all around the country about parents suing recreation departments, schools, and athletic associations because their child did not make the team, did not start a game, or did not make the All-Star roster. We have come to believe that in order for our children to be successful, they must feel successful, whether they are successful or not.

I started noticing this trend when my sister (younger by nine years) began to play recreation department sports. After her last game of the season, her team had a pizza party as a time to gather together and for the families to tell the kids how proud they were of their season. After the team party, she came home and said, "I won a trophy." I was confused. I had never heard of a team winning a trophy for winning only two games. When I asked her what the trophy was for, she answered, "It was for playing the whole season." I learned that the recreation department, like many others all over the country, had given in to the pressure from parents that "everyone should be a winner." This logic says that if everyone wins, kids will not have to feel the hurt or discouragement of losing.

When everyone wins, we all lose.

Winning builds confidence. Losing builds character, inspires perseverance, and causes us to strive even harder.

Some people would fault me here, saying that it is important for kids to win in order to know what winning feels like and to give them the confidence upon which to build a successful life. This chapter is not about winning or losing. It is about the importance of the journey, regardless of the outcome, and the detriment that can be caused by rewarding everyone the same. In life, we succeed and we fail. This is a fact. There are countless stories of very successful people who continually lost; and in that losing, they learned the lessons that shaped them into the people they became. Abraham Lincoln, for instance, lost nine bids for political office before he finally became the President of the United States. It is not only OK, but it is good for kids, and adults for that matter, to feel the pain of defeat and the sting of loss as they go through their life.

Dr. Mel Levine tells us that kids who constantly succeed become increasingly anxious as they grow older, because they do not know how to deal with conflict, obstacles or defeat. When children do not have the "playground defeat" as a learning lab it becomes almost impossible for them to deal with not getting into their first choice college, not landing a great job or not getting a promotion. When we do not allow our kids to lose, we are setting them up for failure for the rest of their lives.

> *"Kids need to feel badly sometimes; we learn through experience and we learn through bad experiences. Through failure we learn how to cope."*—**David Elkind, child psychologist and professor, Tufts University**

THE PARENT TRAP

> *"I wish my parents had some hobby other than me."*[8]
> —**An American teenager**

If this epidemic were to stop at sports, that would be bad enough; unfortunately, it goes far beyond the field. There has been an alarming rise in the pursuit of disability diagnoses from parents so that children can take standardized testing without time limitations. David Anderegg, a child psychologist in Lenox, Massachusetts, and professor of psychology at Bennington College tells us:

> "The kids know when you're cheating on their behalf, and it makes them feel terribly guilty. Sometimes they arrange to fail to right the scales. And when you cheat on their behalf, you completely undermine their sense of self-esteem. They feel they didn't earn it on their own."[9]

Good, well-meaning, loving parents often try to help their kids get ahead but are unintentionally crippling their children with fear and anxiety. Every time parents cheat for their child it not only sets up him or her on false pretenses but also tells the child that he or she is not good enough to do it on his or her own and that the only way to succeed is by riding his or her parents' coattails. This, in turn, is producing a generation of children who, even at 20 years old, have a difficult time operating independently of their parents.

Some are even likening the cell phone to an extended umbilical cord.[10]

I have seen this play out many times on youth group retreats. At one church, we had a student who was attached to his cell phone throughout every retreat. He constantly called his mother to tell her about any part of the trip that he did not like. I received many phone calls from her to "discuss" the details of the trip that her son did not feel comfortable with, such as lights-out times, sleeping arrangements, and even the food. At one point during my tenure at that church, I tried to eliminate cell phones from trips. My hopes were squashed quickly by a few parents because they needed to be able to talk through the different elements of trips with their children to make sure that their kids were having the best time possible.

It was crippling to both the youth and the trip.

TWO WEEKS, FIVE FEET, AND CHARLIE SHEEN

The other effect from this is that the youth again believe that their every emotion is worthy of everyone's immediate attention. This produces something I call the "Two Weeks, Five Feet Rule." The rule is simple: Youth who are parented this way are usually able to see only two weeks out and are concerned only with what is happening with in a five-foot radius of themselves.

Youth are notoriously poor at recognizing the larger picture and the long-term effects of actions. They become exponentially more inept at these practices when the way in which they are raised locates their wants and whims at the center of their parents' functionality. In youth ministry, the practical implications of this sort of thinking are annoying, time consuming, and incredibly frustrating. The real-life implications of two weeks and five feet are devastating to both self and others.

Not too long ago, my wife and I were discussing an interesting issue of *Time* magazine, which featured a cover article heralding the wars over chores among married men and women. The article spent five whole pages discussing the "chore wars" in the American household. When reading the article, you would think that this is a real epidemic. If you flip just a few pages over, there's an article that is more than a little sobering. The article is about Somali refugees fleeing in the midst of drought and famine. These refugees have no home in which to do chores in, much less fight about to whom those chores belong. After being enthralled by the article about chores, I felt humbled to realize how limited my scope of importance was.

We are a nation captivated by the most petty of things. We place massive importance on some of the most inconsequential happenings. While adults are better at long range planning than their youth, the radius of concern is often not much wider.

I was in a session with Mark Oestreicher, veteran youth worker and former president of Youth Specialties, in which he was discussing the elongated adolescence in our society. In his presentation, he talked about how adolescence is lasting into the late twenties and early thirties. This conversation happened during the Charlie Sheen fiasco, so I asked whether this was just indicative of what I was coining the "Charlie Sheen effect." Mark laughed, said that was exactly what was happening and told me that I should copyright that phrase. It is amazing how a man, well into his forties, made $1.8 million an episode by coming to work and acting in front of the camera exactly as he acted in real life: like an angry, hormonalized 16 year old. Please understand me: I am not picking on Charlie Sheen—just the opposite. I am identifying a major shift in our culture. Charlie Sheen is the archetype of elongated adolescence. This example of elongated adolescence has been around for years, but usually as the exception, and has served as comic relief. What the Charlie Sheen effect tells us is that it is no longer the exception to the rule and is also being embraced and glamorized by the general public.

The natural product of parent-trap parenting seems to be a combination of an elongated two weeks, five feet, and the Charlie Sheen effect as well as a country full of young adults who care more about "real housewives" and their fantasy leagues than they do about a Somali refugee.

THE GOSPEL OF ME

The gospel of me says this:

> *"Jesus died for my sins."*

> *"God loved me so much that he sent his only son to die for my sins."*

> *"When Jesus was on the cross, he was thinking about me."*

> The problem with the gospel of me is that it is heretical, because it is all about me.

We have become good of friends with the gospel of me. The gospel of me had its humble roots in the Protestant Reformation. In a time and place where the "self" carried very little importance (in other words, it was all about the church), Martin Luther and his followers began to move the pendulum the other way. I do not think that they intended their efforts to culminate in a gospel of me theology, but they knew that there were personal choices of faith, even interpretation throughout Scripture; and they were not seeing these choices reflected in their church. While there were many other reasons for the Reformation, this foundational concept of the priesthood of all believers seems to be the unintentional great-grandfather of the gospel of me.

Before you string me up and pull out the torches, let me affirm that I completely believe in the priesthood of all believers; it is a core doctrine of my faith, and I could not imagine my spirituality without it. This belief, however, unknowingly became a great tool of modern Christianity's movement toward meism. Where Luther and friends were trying to reform the Catholic Church, they ended up creating more divisions within Christianity. This result set a precedent. When others down the road did not agree with the way the denomination was going, they had the precedent to split and form a sect of the original denomination. The pattern continued so that today we have thousands of Christian denominations in America. Meism has taken something that was necessary in the Reformation and turned it into a self-serving, consumer-driven way to make Church fit my needs.

Again, meism was not the fault of the Reformation but a completely unintended byproduct. The magic really happened when the priesthood of all believers was set up on a date with American consumerism. They fell in love; and before we knew, it we had a little bundle of meism. Our consumerism really was the perfect enabler for the transformation of doctrine of the priesthood of all believers into the gospel of me. It allowed a doctrine that was intended to keep the Pope and the religious aristocracy in check to transform into something that created millions of sovereign papacies, each with his or her own idea of what the gospel is about. Soon verses about God loving the world so much were retranslated into God loving me so much. Our sermons became focused on our personal needs. Our Bible studies focused on self-empowerment. The gospel began to turn inward, and so did our focus.

The gospel of me helps us pick churches based on the music we like, sermons that speak to our lives, and small groups that meet us in our life stages. While all of these things can be strengtheners of our faith, they often end up being the focus points of our faith. The church has found itself in a place where it is more concerned with feeding itself than feeding the world.

> We have become a spiritually obese and gluttonous people.

We build enormous buildings, spend millions of hours in Bible study and worship, and spend comparably very little time and money in taking care of the people Jesus chose to spend most of his ministry with.

Our youth see the church act this way.

Our youth practice this form of religion.

And they are becoming bloated, like the rest of the church.

This is an epidemic, and we must find a cure.

BECOMING HERETICS IN THE CULT OF ME

As I have written this chapter, I have felt really bad. My tone has been preachy; my message, dim.

There is hope.

We have the opportunity to become and create heretics. When people or groups reject the tenets of a religion, they are often labeled heretical. There is a cult of me in our world, and we have the distinct opportunity to lead a religious rebellion against it. We will be labeled heretical, extreme, and even delusional; but we will also find ourselves changing the world and reclaiming the universal scope of our faith.

SUBVERTING THE CULT OF ME

Some foundational pillars that I believe we can build upon as we reform our faith focus not only on the individual but also on how we do this as a community. This is not an exhaustive list, but these four pillars are a starting point from which to launch our revolution.

Pillar 1: Replace 'Me' With 'the World' in Our Theology, Preaching, and Speech

In 2011, some devastating tornadoes ripped through our state and city. Hundreds of people were killed; thousands were displaced and left homeless. In the beginning, agencies were bursting with requests to go in and help. It was beautiful to see so many people want to help. The problem with these sorts of disaster situations is that there is some on-site, ground zero-type work to be done in the beginning; but the majority of it has to be done by professionals with certain skills and safety training. Within a week and a half after the disaster, the majority of the work that could be done was off site, away from ground zero, and usually involved sorting supplies, cooking meals, and packing relief kits. It was not glamorous; it was tedious and it was boring. When agencies would answer phone calls from eager workers and offer these less-than-glamorous jobs, many of the tones changed dramatically. Soon people began to decline this monotonous work, with answers such as (and these are real responses), "I want to do something that I feel good about," "I want to have a meaningful experience," "I want to feel satisfied with the work." For many, the relief effort became more about how they felt while doing the job and less about the importance of the job they were doing.

We have to stop being "pastoral" in these situations and lovingly help people understand that disaster relief is not about how they feel or what they get out of the work. Unfortunately, in the modern church, this switch rarely happens. We have to begin to construct theologies with our youth that regularly put them in unsatisfying situations; assign them work that does not seek to give them a "mission high"; and all along the way, help them understand that the work of God is referred to by Jesus as a cross we are to bear.

The last time I checked, carrying a cross was not very fulfilling, satisfying or a good experience. It is important to reframe our work and mission as something that is much bigger than ourselves, our desires, or our plans. We need to help our students see that God was at work in the situation before we got there and will continue to be at work long after we leave.

This will require a shift in our teaching as well as our actions. Our youth are longing to be called to something beyond themselves; do we have the courage to be the ones calling?

Pillar 2: Bring a Missional Balance to Our Student Ministries

The general purpose of most youth groups in America is to be a place where kids can be accepted, have fun, and be brought up in the ways of their churches. While learning, community, and fun are essential elements of youth group, they have taken the vast majority of our time and resources when compared to the missional aspect of our ministry. What if we were to understand our entire student ministries as missional endeavors? Instead of relegating mission to something we do, what if we were to redesign our ministries so that our theology of mission permeated every piece of our budget, calendar and teaching, worship and activity?

Jesus is our example here. He taught about inclusion; and he practiced it, too. He helped and loved all people. He spent his ministry breaking down political and social barriers that oppressed others.

This missional shift has to be intentional. Our worship has to transform our youth in ways that turn them outward. Our communities have to be inclusive entities. Each line item of our budget has to be examined by the standard of this missional emphasis.

Pillar 3: Redefine the Role of Social Media

Social media is important. It is how we communicate. Unfortunately, our communications have been pretty narrowly focused on ourselves. In the past few years, social media has functioned as sort of global town square. This move has been exhibited no better than in the Middle East. In the Spring of 2011, we saw the rise of the Arab Spring. This series of revolutionary movements in the Middle East was fueled by social media outlets such as Facebook and Twitter. These platforms allowed people to organize and mobilize both effectively and efficiently. The tweets coming out of the Arab Spring had nothing to do with #winning or #Beiber. They were reports of the movement, of encouragements, and of calls to action. Social media was used to get an urgent message instantly delivered to millions of people.

For much of the beginning of the social media revolution, we have called teen usage an addiction. While screen addiction is becoming more prevalent, some believe that their frequency of use point to a deeper need for interaction and belonging.

"Teens aren't addicted to social media. They're addicted to each other.... They're not allowed to hang out the way you and I did, so they've moved it online." [11]

Teens are using social media like a living room, youth room, or ball field. It has become a place where they are escaping into community.

This behavior should be a call to each of us to make social media a place of inclusion, encouragement and communication for the cause of helping others. We live in a time when the quietest among us can spark revolutions, inspire thousands, and change the world. We have seen the YouTube videos of amazing flash mobs. These videos provide incredible entertainment. What if we were to flash mob places of despair, parks whose city cannot pay to have them cleaned, communities that need a helping hand? What if 150 of us were to show up at the same time to do yard maintenance on a city block in disrepair? What if 10 youth groups from across your city were to mob a park full of homeless people and in 10 minutes feed every one of them? These dreams and so many more can become easily realized with just a little initiative and some courageous people who care enough to act.

Pillar 4: Help Parents Land the Chopper

If the National Study of Youth and Religion has taught us anything, it is that we can do very little without the support, encouragement, and enabling of the parents of our youth. One of the trickiest parts of becoming heretics in the cult of me is coming alongside parents and helping them land their helicopters. Plenty of parenting data exists about the dangers of over-parenting that we can use to help our parents. Part of our job, as dangerous as it is, is to help the pendulum swing back from the extremes we have seen in the past decade. If we do not believe that our jobs should include ministering to parents as we minister to their youth, then we are probably in the wrong line of work. Long gone are the days of the One-Eared Mickey Mouse[11] and isolationists youth ministry. I question whether we can even still call it youth ministry. To just call it youth ministry is to deny 70 percent of what the NSYR revealed to us. As we help guide the choppers in, we have to also provide a new model parent ministry for our congregations' families. Some really good resources are already out there on this kind of ministry, but we are still in the earliest stages of this shift in ministry with the church's young people and their families.

We're only in the beginning of the heresies espoused in the cult of me; I hope to hear of more and more communities of heretics springing up all over the country as we reject the false gospel of me and embrace God's concern and love for the world.

1. *Kanye West: God & Monster,* by Mark Beaumont, page 1.
2. NPR Music, "Study: Narcissism on Rise in Pop Lyrics." *http://www.npr.org/2011/04/26/135745227/ study-narcissism-on-rise-in-pop-lyrics.* (Accessed 16 September 2015.)
3. "The Overpraised American," by Christine Rosen, Hoover Institution, Policy Review. *http://www. hoover.org/research/overpraised-american.* (Accessed 16 September 2015.)
4. Pew Research Center's "Teens, Social Media & Technology Overview 2015," by Amanda Lenhart. *http://www.pewinternet.org/2015/04/09/teens-social-media-technology-2015.* (Accessed 16 September 2015.)
5. "Youth Culture Window," by David R. Smith. *http://www.thesource4ym.com/youthculturewindow/ article.aspx?ID=295.* (Accessed 16 September 2015.)
6. "A Nation of Wimps," by Hara Estroff Marano, *Psychology Today,* Nov. 1, 2004. *http://www. psychologytoday.com/articles/200411/nation-wimps.* (Accessed 16 September 2015.)
7. "A Nation of Wimps," Marano.
8. "A Nation of Wimps," Marano.
9. "A Nation of Wimps," Marano.
10. "New Research About Teens, Social Media, & What They Need From Us: Not as Complicated as It Seems," by Art Bamford, Fuller Youth Institute. *http://fulleryouthinstitute.org/blog/ new-research-about-teens-social-media-what-they-need-from-us#sthash.jm0yZrw1.dpuf-.* (Accessed 16 September 2015.)
11. The "One-Eared Mickey Mouse" is a concept developed by Stuart Cummings-Bond and widely popularized by Kenda Creasy Dean in *The Godbearing Life.* This concept says that most youth ministries function like a one-eared Mickey Mouse. They are loosely connected to the larger church and act as largely independent body.

5

THE GREAT DEFICIT
OF HAVING EVERYTHING

"Mass consumer capitalism constitutes the human self in a very particular way: as an individual, autonomous, rational, self-seeking, cost benefit calculating consumer. This, of course, is not what human selves have always been, nor what they must inevitably be."[1]—**Christian Smith, Soul Searching, on mass consumer capitalism**

A few years ago, my wife and I decided to downgrade our lifestyle. I had accepted a new student ministry position, which required us to move from Atlanta to Birmingham. We had lived in Atlanta for five years in a nice middle-sized house. Although we had accumulated a lot of stuff, we still had plenty of room. We never felt cramped or overwhelmed by our possessions.

Then we started packing; and all of a sudden, we realized just how much stuff we had. This was exacerbated by the fact that we were planning to move into two bedrooms in my wife's grandfather's house for an indefinite time as we waited on our house to sell. We knew that we had to scale down big time. We gave away about a third of our belongings. It was difficult at first. I could not get my wife to understand why I needed six packs of playing cards to go along with $2.2 million in poker chips. I thought that it was an absolute need, considering that I had invited friends over to play poker at least once the five years we'd live in the house. I even pulled out the old Boy Scout motto, "Always be prepared." It did not work.

The pain subsided the more we gave away, and giving away became therapeutic. All of us realized how much we had and how little we needed. During the three years since the move, we have given away about two-thirds of our belongings; and our whole family looks forward to our quarterly purging sessions. We are recovering "material-holics."

> Materialism is a value system that emphasizes wealth, status, image, and material consumption. It is a measure of how much we value material things over other things in our lives, such as friends, family and work.[2]

It really is amazing just how easy it is to find ourselves buried under piles of useless things or even useful things we do not need. When we go to a fast-food place, both of our kids get a new toy with their meal. I go to conferences and come home with all sorts of swag. We buy things that are on sale whether we need them or not because "it's a deal." Christmas comes around and we all know nothing says "Happy birthday, Baby Jesus" like thousands of pounds of stuff that none of us need. We are under constant bombardment from television, radio, billboards, magazines, Internet, and so forth, telling us all of the things we need that we do not already have. We are a country of addiction—addiction to stuff.

Our addiction to stuff fuels our addiction to money. An annual study[3] of incoming college freshmen conducted by UCLA found a dramatic shift in our youth's reason for attending college. In the 1960s and 1970s most students placed the highest value on "becoming an educated person" and "developing a philosophy of life" for their reason for attending college. A dramatic shift came in the 1990s, when a majority of students' primary reason for attending college was "making a lot of money." Kids are the natural heirs of their parents' upward mobility. Success has been defined in monetary and materialistic terms, as we are a nation of very successful people.

KIDS WHO HAVE EVERYTHING NEED NOTHING, INCLUDING GOD

Yesterday's luxuries become today's necessities.[4]
—Madeline Levine, Ph.D., *The Price of Privilege*

Oh, for the good old days when people would stop
Christmas shopping when they ran out of money.
—Author Unknown

We have reinterpreted our love for stuff into a new form of love. How do we show others that we love them? We give them gifts: birthdays, holidays, when we have wronged someone, when a friend has accomplished something great. We show affection to others by giving them things.

I see this around graduation season, and it amazes me. I know many families who spend a small fortune on graduation gifts for people they barely know. This phenomenon is at its worst at Christmas. If you took an hour's worth of television as the standard for how to celebrate the holidays, you would have to buy a Lexus with a ridiculously large bow, several diamond pendants, and hundreds of other items that apparently tell someone special that you love him or her. Our country has been seduced into believing that giving a gift is the best, and maybe only, way to tell someone that you love him or her.

> By the looks of our credit card statements and
> attics, we love our kids a lot.

Not only has buying stuff been translated into a form of love, it has also become a form of satisfaction and therapy among many Americans. The acquisition of goods has become something by which we define ourselves. Jewelry shows the world that we are special, cars say that we are powerful, colognes say that we are desirable, and laundry detergent says that we have no other care in the world but the smell of a mid-summer breeze. Advertisers have become so good that they do not even have to talk about their actual product in their ads. Beer commercials are especially good at this. Remember "Bud-weis-errrrrrr"? Those three talking frogs took the world by storm, and they had nothing to do with the product. Now you see entire beer commercials about the wide mouth can, the spiral neck, or that Rocky Mountain experience you have when drinking their product. You crack open a couple of these cans and instantly a dragging, hot summer's day turns into a cool beach party. It's amazing! Or so they would have us believe.

Why do we work so hard to buy so much stuff that we so desperately do not need? Madeline Levine writes about the phenomenon:

> *Because advertising is designed to first make us feel insecure and then solve our insecurity by offering products, it is particularly problematic for adolescents, who already feel terribly insecure.* [5]

These insecurities are preyed upon, targeted and exploited. Then the companies who exploited the insecurities swoop in and offer their products as the solution. The problem arises when that new car doesn't get us the promotion, the diamond ring does not fix the marriage, and the wallflower's phone's contact list is still empty. Adults and youth then are left on an endless search for fulfillment and satisfaction. They flit from one product to the next, hoping that it will define (or redefine) them into the people they see in the advertisements. It becomes a strange rhythm where the prescribed medicine continues to not work but we continue to shell out billions of dollars a year hoping that something will change.

Jesus dealt with this. There once was a rich young person. He knew that the medicine was not working and came to Jesus asking what would work. Jesus told him to flush the pills (give away your possessions) and follow me. The text then says that the rich young man did not say a word and walked away sadly. It was not the rich young man's stuff that was his problem; it was his attitude toward his stuff that made the difference. It is interesting how relevant this 2,000 year old story is in the conversation about today's youth and their possessions. Our youth have been fooled into believing that their possessions define them, and consequently, they spend their lives chasing an imaginary carrot that cannot be caught.

So much of the problem of religious apathy in youth is that so many of them see Christianity as another product. I have talked with so many youth who describe their faith in the same way they describe playing football or the cello. It's an addition that enhances their lives. It is another product that they hope will add to the patchwork of their persona. Like any product that is advertised to them, if it does not "work" for them, they will move on to the next one that promises to deliver the results. One of the reasons modern religion seems to stick a little longer in the world of persona add-ons is that it comes with some implicit social benefits—or it used to. With religion becoming less a part of our social contract, the adherence and association with religion is also losing appeal. This makes complete sense when religion is used as an enhancer.

RALPHIE'S LITTLE BROTHER'S WINTER COAT

"Mom! (sniffling and whimpering) I can't put my arms down!"—Randy Parker, Ralphie's little brother, in *A Christmas Story*

Every Christmas season, I watch the modern classic *A Christmas Story*. I watch it over and over; I cannot seem to get enough of it. It is really an amazing holiday tradition in my home. There are so many memorable scenes: the lamp, the flagpole, Peking duck for Christmas dinner. One scene makes me lose it every time. It has been snowing, and Ralphie and Randy's mom is packing them into their winter clothes for the trek to school. In a hilarious montage where the mom adds layer after suffocating layer to Randy for his supposed protection from the cold, the scene ends in Randy's proclamation of "Mom! I can't put my arms down!" His mom replies, "Well, you can put them down when you get to school."

I think that we and our youth are a lot like Randy and his mom. We know that it is a cold, harsh, dangerous world out there; and we want to insulate our kids as much as possible, in the hope that they will not have to experience the harsh reality of the world outside our home. This second phenomenon of consumerism in our culture is that we use consumerism as an insulator. We surround ourselves with more and more items to insulate ourselves from being alone, doing without, and seeming needy and vulnerable. I so often see youth having things just so that they can be a part of the club that has those items. They surround themselves with these items, hoping to have something in common, something tangible that says, "I am a part of the group and protected from the elements of not belonging." Our culture has done so much of this shielding that our youth are becoming immobilized by their possessions, by the very things they think will protect them and promise to give them freedom. This behavior is such a phenomenon that American teenagers spend $170 billion annually of their own money and

THE GREAT DEFICIT OF HAVING EVERYTHING

around $500 billion of their parents' money.[6] The immobilization occurs from the anxiety that they will not be able to continue to be on the cutting edge of whatever it is that brings them identity and belonging. They become trapped by the constant perceived need for more and newer products.

The result of Smith's study reveals the heart of a teenager, one that has been covered up by a thirst for possessions. My concern is, what happens when we help students sift through their materialistic quest? What do they uncover underneath the pile of things they've acquired? I believe that youth are afraid of what they might find if they were to strip away all of their possessions. Many youth have spent so much time using stuff to create their personas that they might not recognize the person they find underneath. Think about the guy who has built his whole reputation on being "the guy with the car" or the girl whose outfits keep others at arm's length. Think about the Goth kid without the Goth or the tech kid without the tech. I hope that in youth ministry, we are imagining or will begin to imagine our kids in these ways. I often find myself falling into their trap, perceiving kids based on what they have or what they do not have. We have a very important job of helping to de-insulate little Randy Parker and help him move freely again.

LEPROSY AND THE GIFT OF PAIN

"Most people view pain as an enemy. Yet, as my leprosy patients prove, it forces us to pay attention to threats against our bodies. Without it heart attacks, strokes, ruptured appendixes, and stomach ulcers would all occur without any warning. Who would ever visit a doctor apart from pain's warnings?"[7]—**Dr. Paul Brand, from** *Soul Survivor*

One of the books I go back to time and time again when I'm in need of healing is a faith journey memoir by Phillip Yancey called *Soul Survivor*. The book chronicles the people who influenced Yancey most profoundly through his faith journey. The most beautiful entry is about Dr. Paul Brand, who was born in the early twentieth century to missionary parents in India. While in India, the young Brand regularly experienced leprosy firsthand in his community. Later in life, as a distinguished doctor, Brand decided to forgo prestigious appointments for the slums and leper colonies of India. During his time, he sought to gain more understanding about the mysterious disease. Through his research, he found that leprosy was not the actual cause of the rotting of the victims' flesh. He discovered that the disease attacked the nerve endings and caused the patient an inability to feel. This inability to feel then made the patient much more susceptible to injury, infection, and eventually the loss of appendages. Dr. Brand helped us understand that pain is a beautiful gift that many of us never recognize as such.

Pain is recognition of our ability to feel.

Unfortunately, many in our culture believe that it is better to be a leper, to live without feeling. The loss of feeling, especially when that feeling is pain, is a chronic disease affecting our youth.

If you spend any time at all with parents and their youth, you will see the promotion of this affliction of living without feeling. As a parent, I completely understand why. As I write this, just one hour ago, I sent my little girl off to Kindergarten for her very first day of school. I cannot tell you the massive amount of anxiety I felt as I walked her to the door of her school, kissed her, and sent her off on her own. I wanted so badly to protect her from hurt, bullying, rejection, fear, anxiety, sadness, failure,—anything that could possibly take away that innocent excitement streaming across her beautiful face. Fortunately, I know that all of those things, in balance with the good stuff, make her stronger, more confident, and aware. I know that she has to fail; to feel sadness, heartbreak, indecision, anxiety, and even rejection. If I were to let my own anxiety and fear take over, I would try to insulate her from these things. Some kid will have a cooler backpack or lunch box, another might make better grades, and another might have better clothes.

I remember being in middle school and never really having the best, coolest, or newest anything. (Well, that was how it felt to me.) I had to learn to not build my identity around and put my trust in those "cool" things. It became less important to have those things. It took time and was frequently very painful. Yet I began to realize that I had what I needed and that my self-worth and identity were derived from other things. It took pain and sometimes embarrassment to get there, but I survived—even when I thought that I might die on the spot. It is amazing how feeling pain, even if now it seems insignificant, was so important. One of the most hurtful things we can do to our children and our youth is to protect them with such comfort that they never have the joy of feeling—even if that feeling sometimes comes in the form of pain.

GIVING GIFTS THAT DO NOT RUST

"But I was caught in between all you wish for and all you need."—Joseph Arthur, from his song "In the Sun"

My father-in-law was in the Navy. He was an engineer on a nuclear submarine. He sometimes jokes about how the military takes everything away when you join. He says that when he was in a situation where he was being made to feel like a peon, he could think to himself, "Well, at least you can't take away my birthday!" I laugh so hard when I think of this, but it also makes me remember that there are gifts that cannot be taken away from our youth. Earlier, I almost made an enemy of the idea of giving as a form of love. I want to rectify and modify that idea a little. Giving can be a wonderful way to show love. We give others our trust, our compassion, our forgiveness, and our companionship when we love them. In a marriage, we give our entire self to our partner in trust and love. Even the root of our theology recognizes Jesus' death as a gift to all of humanity. Gifts can be a beautiful way to show love. We as parents and youth ministers have the distinct opportunity to show our love to our youth by giving some of these intangible gifts.

One of the most important of the gifts that we can give is when we model a different way of understanding possessions by practicing and modeling the disciplines of simplicity, gratitude, and generosity.

GIVING INTANGIBLE GIFTS

"Effective contestation [of hyper-consumptive culture] can have a profound impact on the spiritual formation of our children, and should be considered a worthy social ministry by parents and communities of faith."[8]
—Katherine Turpin, "Princess Dreams," from *Children, Youth, and Spirituality in a Troubling World*

Unfortunately the word *materialism* carries so much baggage and is so varied by our understanding of our own context that it is difficult to have any sort of a clear conversation about it without wanting to give up and retreat. So instead of attacking how much we have or what is the quality of product we consume, I think that we can work at it from a different perspective. Instead of talking just about what we have in a negative way, I propose that we think about what we can possess or embody in a positive way. Here are three "gifts" we can claim as our own that we can give to one another and to the world.

Simplicity

Simplicity is a concept that has gained significant recognition in the past few years. Simplicity encompasses everything from the green movement, to food and the way we eat, to religious communities such as The Simple Way. I think that this is why the nature of marketing has intensified so significantly in recent years. Some of the best marketing strategies are capitalizing on these movements to buy even more of their product. In its best most biblical form, simplicity takes on a different approach than these marketing strategies. Simplicity in its purest version is just that—simple. Simplicity means less clutter, less mess, and less obligation to keep up with material stuff. As a nation of consumers, we base most of our choices on convenience, simplicity, and intentionality call us to make more responsible decisions, which are not always the easiest or most convenient. This is one of the most difficult things for me to model in my ministry. I love having loads of options for our kids. Full programs with loads of different tracks have been an important aspect of my youth ministry programming for so long. I have had to rethink what this strategy is telling my youth. I have come to believe that having too much and too many options is creating for them a certain Christian subculture that encourages the "waffle effect" in their lives. Simplicity can act as both the fuel for and the method by which to make this transition.

Gratitude

Another intangible gift we can give students is the gift of gratitude. It is astounding how little gratitude we encounter on a daily basis. This is very evident to me when I am driving and I am so surprised when someone gives me a subtle wave to thank me for letting them in the traffic line. It happens so rarely that I want to stop and give them a hug and thank them for thanking me. Unfortunately, this simple, cordial act has become the exception; so we hold it as some sort of high standard for gratitude.

Gratitude is not only being thankful for what is given but also for what we already have. We live in a time and place where upward mobility and upgrades are expected, not an exciting exception. This ingrained belief that we should constantly be on the lookout for something better has destroyed the entire concept of gratitude. We have such an opportunity to model this for our students. Whether it is being publicly thankful or privately grateful this attitude can have a great impact on them. Another way to demonstrate gratitude to our students is to slow down and recognize people as people. When I say "as people," I mean as beloved children of God. In ministry, it is so easy to slip into the trap of seeing volunteers, students, and parents as commodities with varying values. Often without even knowing it, we place value on them by what they "do" for us. In *The Price of Privilege,* Madeline Levine writes:

"At worst, materialism turns our most valued relationships into commodities."[9]

If you're anything like me, that stabs right through your heart and the heart of how you practice ministry. Most of the time, we don't realize that we've made the shift from relationship to commodity. Valuing everyone, no matter their ministerial worth, participation level, or monetary or influential wealth is one of the most powerful ways to model gratitude for our youth.

Generosity

Finally, we have to model generosity. We cannot limit our understanding of generosity to money alone, however. We have to also be generous with our love, time, patience, and grace. We must model generosity with our abilities and gifts. Helping people explore, discover, and develop their naturally occurring gifts and strengths can be a wonderful example to set for our youth. In a church culture where youth are often marginalized because of their perceived inability to contribute, this generosity of talents can make huge inroads into service and even leadership in an often closed church culture. Preaching, teaching, and developing small groups about these practices can do only so much. Our youth look to us as examples for how to practice the faith, so we must be the living examples they need in order to become people who live out generosity, gratitude, and simplicity.

1. *Soul Searching*, Smith, page 176.
2. *The Price of Privilege*, by Madeline Levine, page 45.
3. The American Freshman; National Norms for Fall 1998 (Annual: Higher Education Research Institute; Los Angeles: University of California), L. Sax, et al (1998). *http://heri.ucla.edu/pr-display. php?prQry=22.* (Accessed 16 September 2015.)
4. *The Price of Privilege*, Levine, page 48.
5. *The Price of Privilege*, Levine, page 51.
6. *Soul Searching*, Smith, page 178.
7. *Soul Survivor: How Thirteen Unlikely Mentors Helped My Faith Survive the Church*, by Phillip Yancey, page 72.
8. Katherine Turpin, "Princess Dreams," in *The Price of Privilege*, ed. by Almeda Wright and Dr. Mary Elizabeth Moore, page 61.
9. *The Price of Privilege*, Levine, page 48.

BEING AUTHENTICALLY CHRISTIAN IN A POST-GOOGLE WORLD

THE TIMES THEY HAVE A-CHANGED

> *Come gather 'round people*
> *Wherever you roam*
> *And admit that the waters*
> *Around you have grown*
> *And accept it that soon*
> *You'll be drenched to the bone*
> *If your time to you is worth savin'*
> *Then you better start swimmin' or you'll sink like a stone*
> *For the times they are a-changin'."*

—Bob Dylan, "The Times They Are A-Changin'"[1]

When Bob Dylan penned his classic, "The Times They Are A-Changin'" in 1963, he was surrounded by numerous instances of inspiration. From the Vietnam War to the Civil and Women's Rights movements, things were changing all around the young singer/songwriter. When asked about the song, he said that he was writing an anthem of change for the movement that was going on around him. It is a ballad that has just as much meaning in our current religio-cultural context now as it did in Dylan's social context. The water is rising, and people of faith have to decide whether to swim or sink like a stone; because the times they are a-changin'.

One of my graduate school professors, Dr. Graham Walker, once lectured about the dramatic shift in theological thinking after the Holocaust. "We used to think about having to do post-Holocaust theology; now we have to think about what it means to learn to do Google theology."

I remember traveling encyclopedia salesmen. They would come and tell us about all of the amazing knowledge we could obtain through the many volumes of the Encyclopedia Britannica. I remember how amazing it was that so much information could be right there on three or four shelves in my living room. What I realize now is that information was long outdated by the time that salesman knocked on my door. And it was big and clunky. In a Google world, we have a million times the amount of information of the Encyclopedia Britannica; it's constantly being updated; and it also just happens to be in my pocket, right there beside Angry Birds.

Amazing.

Many historians note that the most dramatic and seismic global, societal and cultural shifts are fueled by new, more-efficient ways to communicate information to the masses. No tool in history has done that more effectively than the Internet and its primary information aggregator, Google. Not only can I know what is going on almost anywhere in the world at any given moment, I can also see and interact with those events. In addition to how we receive our news and information, how we experience and understand our fellow humans has shifted drastically. Where once we only heard stories of the Bushmen of Africa, we can now see them live-streamed on our computers; or we can watch shows where people just like us go to live with the Bushmen and learn their ways and culture. Through this technology, we are experiencing people and their faiths in whole new ways as well.

BIG LESSONS FROM A SMALL, SMALL WORLD

"The world is not getting so small that there is room for only one story."[2]—**Doreen Massey, professor of geography at Open University**

When I go to theme parks, there are two types of rides that I frequent. The first are the popular roller coasters, theme rides, and anything that will be wildly entertaining. The second sort of ride is much different, the air conditioned ones. Every major theme park knows that you have to have these rides available all over the park as a respite from the extreme heat and humidity of the summer tourist season. The park I grew up going to in Atlanta had the Monster Plantation, a fun and relatively long ride where I could enjoy air conditioning for about 10 minutes. Disney World in Orlando has a myriad of these rides, none, however, are as well-known as "It's a Small World." The ride is a "cruise" through every continent and the cultures of that continent. There are hundreds of these animatronic dolls singing the theme song about its being a "small, small world."

When Disney created this ride in the 1970s, I'm sure they had no clue just how small of a world it would become.

As the world has become smaller, our access to knowledge and our technological scope has grown. While the Internet has made the possibility of our connections and knowledge increase exponentially, what happened on September 11, 2001, made many of those possibilities everyday realities. While we could learn about other cultures and religions from websites and blogs, 9/11 forced our nation into an inter-cultural, inter-religious quest for understanding and, in its best forms, dialogue. For most Americans, the discussions of the intersections between Christianity and Islam would no longer live in theoretical realms. While the foundational tenets that fueled the hijackers were no more an image of Islam than the Third Reich were manifestations of Christianity, the tragedy did propel all of us into a deeply personal interaction with a religion many of us knew little about.

Our world became a lot smaller.

We saw several reactions to this change in the days after September 11. Some people immediately went to the Internet to try to understand Islam. Others went to places of worship and processed through these events with clergy (both peace-seeking and inflammatory) and congregations. Some resorted to violence and began to target those who may have been of a Middle Eastern lineage. Still others gathered with people of other faith traditions, such as Jews and Muslims, and bound themselves together in prayer and unity. There were many reactions to that immediate change in our world; those reactions have now turned into dogmas for most.

BEYOND FALWELL AND BIN LADEN

"You must not consider tolerance and patience to be signs of weakness. I consider them signs of strength."[3]—*Dalai Lama*

In times of extreme fear, humanity begins to polarize. Many believe that this is an ingrained primitive survival instinct. The rationale is that when threatened, the individual places itself diametrically opposed to the thing it feels is threatening it in order to preserve its life. We have seen this manifestation in modern history. When you look at the events and groups in modern conflicts, especially during times of scarcity, polarizations appear quickly and strongly. Think about the internment camps of the Second World War, the Red Scare, McCarthyism, the American Civil Rights movement, or our current political climate. It seems more than natural for humans to be drawn to an extreme during these times of fear and uncertainty. There is another way, a better way.

Although there are many models for handling different ideologies, the following three stand out to me as predominant reactions to our current pluralistic climate, the first two being the most common.

The First Way: The Crusades—Conquest and Conquer

The Crusades were the bloody, religiously-sanctioned military campaigns, or "holy wars," that occurred between 1095 and 1291. These wars were primarily fought between Roman Catholics and Muslim groups over control of Jerusalem and the rest of the holy lands. While these wars were religious, they were certainly geo-political in nature and scope. I do not want to debate the reasons for the conflict here but would rather focus on the vehicle by which these differences were solved.

There are two words that come to my mind when I think about the Crusades: *conquest* and *conquer*. The Crusades were battles over land, and he who had the land won the war. The way each group chose to pursue this victory was to constantly be on the offensive pushing the other group back and taking the land for themselves. This strategy sounds like the way many Christians approach our ever-increasing pluralistic world.

There seems to be a conquest-flavored blood thirst for many churches and religious groups to completely take the land by way of the sword. Sometimes this takeover is executed by way of evangelism. Other times, it happens under the banner of public policy. No matter the vehicle, many have approached the changing religious landscape, believing that the only way to survive is to constantly gain ground and make sure that the other is losing ground. After 2001, this attitude was a major way of functioning for many who call themselves Christian. While Qur'an burning and violence are the exceptions, there is a fundamental fear, suspicion, and hostility from the American church toward Muslims. Forty-three percent of Americans admit to carrying some sort of prejudice against Muslims.[3] Much of the rhetoric not only distorts the tenets of Islam but is simply unfounded and is being used as political and ideological fodder, not only against Muslims but against an increasingly pluralistic society.

The Second Way: The School of Athens—Discuss and Debate

Raphael's painting *The School of Athens* is one of my favorite frescos in the entire world. Twice in my life, I have been fortunate to sit before it in the Vatican and have continued to be in awe of its balance, beauty, and depth. Within the painting are various academic figures throughout history, discussing, debating, and even arguing their points to and against the other scholars. It's fun to go through and pick out the various scholars represented in the painting, from Socrates to Pythagoras. So many recognizable figures fill the steps of this great work of art. The focal point of the piece is Plato and Aristotle walking and debating. Plato points up, explaining his ideology that the answer is found in the archetypes; while Aristotle points down, defending his philosophy that what matters are the tangibles, the things present.

Many Christians interact with a pluralistic culture by discussing and debating our differences. This is not a bad thing. We are different in many ways from other religions. It's very helpful to enter into wholesome and good-natured discussions about faith and how that faith is lived out. If more people were to practice the art of discussion—listening as much as we speak—we would have a greater understanding and appreciation of other religions. While the *School of Athens* method is helpful and not violent, it still lacks two important elements. First, the thing that brings us together is debating of our differences. Simply being together is not enough. There has to be something more in common than the things that we do not have in common. The second is that there's nothing uniquely Christian about just coming together. While it is good, it is still lacking.

The Third Way: Convivencia—Coexist and Collaborate

La Convivencia was the culmination of a region, period, and ideology that exited in Spain between A.D. 700 and 1400. This almost mythical community was a learning, cultural, and art hub for Christians, Jews, and Muslims. The idea that permeated La Convivencia was not only to live in peace but to work, create, and learn from one another. This area became a place where cultures came together and focused on what they had in common, instead of how they differed. The idea was that they could collaborate and coexist while at the same time remain faithful to their belief and practice it openly. The existence and proximity of other ideologies was not a threat but a place from which to learn and develop cross cultural and religious relationships. I believe that this understanding, when applied to our increasingly pluralistic society, not only makes sense but can be understood as uniquely Christian in nature.

HOSPITALITY, LOVE, AND SAMARITANISM AS AN UNIQUELY CHRISTIAN ANSWER TO PLURALISM

"Which one of these three was a neighbor to the man who encountered thieves?" Then the legal expert said, "The one who demonstrated mercy toward him." Jesus told him, "Go and do likewise."—Luke 10:36-37

It was understood that during La Convivencia, the participants' depth of relationship exceeded mere toleration. Participants were to make an intentional effort toward authentic community. The term *La Convivencia* is literally translated as "the coexistence." Some scholars will argue that the idea of this community has been blown out of proportion and has even reached mythological status. I, however, am not basing my idea here on whether or not the details of the actual community are absolutely accurate; I am basing it purely on the idea of La Convivencia. This is not to say that the history is not important. I believe that it, like many teachings that call us beyond ourselves and our current contexts and practices, is not invalid just because it has not yet been achieved. So while the realization of this community historically may have a haze of mythos surrounding it, I believe that we can still use its core tenets and ideas as a basis to practice hospitality in a pluralistic society.

I don't believe that this idea was invented in the eighth century. Throughout Scripture, the tenets of hospitality and love are held in places of prominence, especially when referring to how a follower of God interacts with strangers, both enemy and alien. In both the Hebrew Bible as well as the New Testament, we see countless stories of God commending those who made it their habit to treat the "other" with hospitality and love.

Christian hospitality and love are both exemplified in the story of the Samaritan and the beaten and abandoned Jew. We know that Samaritans and Jews were at odds both racially and religiously. They were both laying claim to the God of Abraham but were doing so in very different geographic and cultural ways. They had a historically bitter dispute over who were the true worshippers of the God of Abraham. The argument put these two groups at great odds with each other. By the time Jesus was on the scene, they had become each other's worst enemies.

In walks a Jew
He is beaten, robbed, left for dead,
Not only left by the robbers but by his
    own people
In walks a Samaritan
He not only stopped,
He helped, took on his burden
Physically,
Financially,
In the eyes of his enemies
And his peers
And their God.

When I see this interaction, I cannot help but believe that Jesus is telling his followers that there is a third way of dealing with people of different, opposite, and conflicting faiths. Through this story, Jesus is calling us to care for one another's burdens and needs. What more is community than sharing one another's burdens, needs, and cares?

Our religious, social, and political climates have tried to put Christians and Jews at odds with Muslims, in many ways like the Jews and Samaritans were divided for hundreds of years. All three religions lay claim to the God of Abraham, common geographical interests, as well as the problem of their bitter disputes and attacks over which is the one true religion of the Abrahamic faiths. This time, instead of being on a regional scale, we find the divide on a global stage. Jesus had words for such divisions, and they are just as pertinent today as they were thousands of years ago.

Our youth are in a place that neither we nor any other society has experienced. Not only are they experiencing people of many different faiths in person, they are also exposed to beliefs of all kinds through the connectional powers of the Internet and television. They are experiencing people and faiths who are genuine and real, and many of them have been brought up to believe that the only way to interact with these faiths is in a combative or argumentative manner. We have a distinct opportunity to model a new way based on the Christian principles of hospitality and love, practiced as a part of and not in spite of our faith.

We will have to deal with pluralism delicately and with great compassion. Two ways we can tread down these roads while being uniquely Christian in our belief and practice: through education and working toward a common goal.

Education

In the winter of my sophomore year of college, I and thirteen other students and four professors spent a month in Jordan and Syria studying Islam. It was my first time to fly, much less go to a region so different from my own. The experience was transformative. One of the most helpful parts of the trip was the man I sat next to on the plane. My seat was away from the other students on the trip; I sat beside a Jordanian-born doctor. Abrahim and I introduced ourselves early in the flight; and before I could stop myself, I was asking him questions about his faith, how his people saw Americans, what he thought about Jesus and Christians. At one point on our 17-hour flight, he smiled and told me, "Your teacher must rest; we will resume class after a short nap." He was more than generous with a wide-eyed 20 year old from rural Alabama. I learned so much. I learned about a real Muslim's faith, not what was in a book or on the news. I learned how his family and everyday life was very much like mine. I learned how our hopes and desires were so similar and how we had so much in common.

We need to help students engage in these kind of conversations. Books and reports will take us only so far. Jesus and the Samaritan woman are a good example. The woman was shocked that Jesus, a Jew, would speak to her, a Samaritan woman (John 4:9). Jesus knew and practiced what it meant to be in relationship with the other. Was Jesus any less of a faithful Jew because he was in community with this woman? This education is just as much about re-humanization as it is about knowledge. It is amazing what sharing a meal can do to make friends out of strangers.

Working Toward a Common Goal

Eboo Patel is an American Muslim of Gujarati Indian heritage and founder and president of the Interfaith Youth Core, a Chicago-based international nonprofit that aims to promote interfaith cooperation.[3] He understands the idea of a common purpose and goal that brings people of all faiths together. Eboo came to believe that we can come together and find more in common that we find in conflict, so he developed the idea of IFYC. Their guiding principles say this:

Muslims and Hindus, Jews and Christians, Buddhists and non-religious are coming together in a movement of interfaith cooperation. They are proving that the twenty-first century can be defined by cooperation between diverse communities, instead of conflict.

What a beautiful way to understand and participate in our ever-changing pluralistic world. They are doing this with college and high school students all over the nation. The current campaign is called "Better Together," echoing that when stand together, we can do greater things than when we are apart. IFYC does not ask people to check their faith or beliefs at the door; they encourage people to be uniquely themselves. This sounds encouragingly similar to what Jesus seemed to be alluding to when he made reference to and practiced the signs of the kingdom of God.

We have the opportunity to lead in this beautifully Christian response to our pluralistic world. Keeping and practicing our uniquely

Christian faith, learning and appreciating the other great faiths of the world, and joining with them to make this world a better place.

La Convivencia.

1. "The Times They Are A-Changin'," by Bob Dylan. Copyright © 1963, 1964 by Warner Bros. Inc.; renewed 1991, 1992 by Special Rider Music. Used by permission. All rights reserved.
2. "Is the World Getting Larger or Smaller?" by Doreen Massey. *https://www.opendemocracy.net/globalization-vision_reflections/world_small_4354.jsp*. (Accessed 17 September 2015.)
3. *An Open Heart: Practicing Compassion in Everyday Life,* by The Dalai Lama, page 21.
4. "In U.S., Religious Prejudice Stronger Against Muslims," analysis by the Gallup Center for Muslim Studies. *http://www.gallup.com/poll/125312/religious-prejudice-stronger-against-muslims.aspx*. (Accessed 16 September 2015.)
4. Interfaith Youth Core. *http://www.ifyc.org/about-us/eboo-patel*. (Accessed 16 September 2015.)

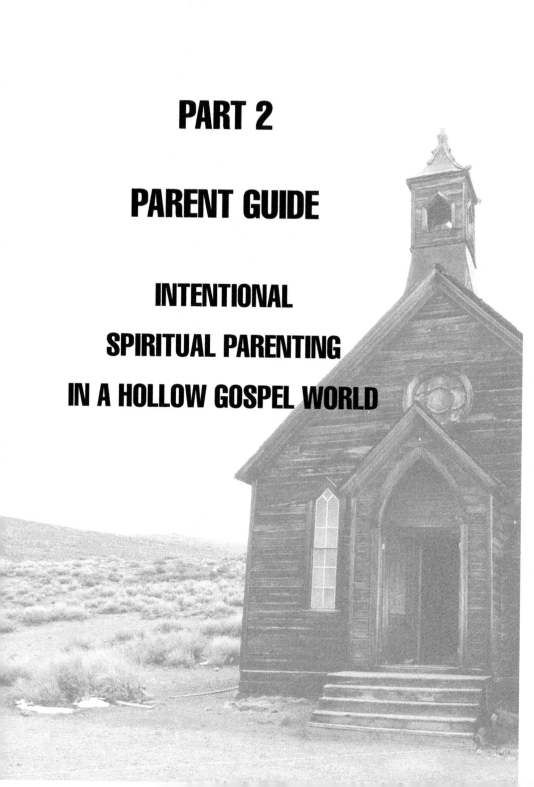

PART 2

PARENT GUIDE

INTENTIONAL
SPIRITUAL PARENTING
IN A HOLLOW GOSPEL WORLD

INTRODUCTION

This section introduces, in brief, some conversations to begin to
have with parents and families, based on the discussions found in
this book. These dialogues will include the theoretical discussions
and some practical jumping-off points for families to begin to
implement a familial flow and rhythm change. This change in not
only understanding but actual practice is intended to reshape how
we understand and practice our relationships with God, stranger,
and self. These points are not meant to be the end-all practices for
bringing about these sorts of systemic changes in our families' lives.
These discussions are simply starting blocks meant to be a solid
foundational piece from which to begin conversations and practices
that the student ministry and church as a whole can then begin to
form shape and build from. The individual churches will have to
imagine, create, and practice pieces that come from the marriage of
these foundational pieces and the DNA of the ecclesial body.

Isn't That What We Hired the Youth Minister for?

If nothing else has been learned over the past ten years of youth
ministry research, we now know through empirical evidence what
practical evidence has been telling us since the foundations of the
world: Parents are the most essential forces in a child's life, spirituality,
and future—something that can no longer be ignored in ministry with
youth. It feels like forever ago that Kenda Creasy Dean was drawing
one-eared Mickey Mouses on white boards to help us understand the
importance of student ministries being fully rooted in the life of the
church; now we are going even further, having to understand student
ministries as being fully ingrained in the families and vice versa.
There has been some push back to this understanding: The common
refrain from student ministers is, "Kids do not want their parents
too involved; that's what we are for." And the parents respond with,

"Isn't that the youth minister's job? My kids are not going to talk with me about that stuff; and even if they did, I do not know enough about the Bible to help them." The time for heeding these warnings is over, and the time to dispel these myths and enable families to be the primary place of spiritual nurture and growth is upon us.

As for Me and My House . . .

There are countless biblical examples for understanding ministry with youth as ministry with families, and very few or none at all for stand-alone ministry with youth. One of the best-known stories in this understanding is when Paul and Silas encounter the jailer at the midnight hour.

> Around midnight Paul and Silas were praying and singing hymns to God, and the other prisoners were listening to them. All at once there was such a violent earthquake that it shook the prison's foundations. The doors flew open and everyone's chains came loose. When the jailer awoke and saw the open doors of the prison, he thought the prisoners had escaped, so he drew his sword and was about to kill himself. But Paul shouted loudly, "Don't harm yourself! We're all here!"
>
> The jailer called for some lights, rushed in, and fell trembling before Paul and Silas. He led them outside and asked, "Honorable masters, what must I do to be rescued?"
>
> They replied, "Believe in the Lord Jesus, and you will be saved—you and your entire household." They spoke the Lord's word to him and everyone else in his house. Right then, in the middle of the night, the jailer welcomed them and washed their wounds. He and everyone in his household were immediately baptized. He brought them into his home and gave them a meal. He was overjoyed because he and everyone in his household had come to believe in God. (Acts 16:25-34)

This verse reflects the continued biblical narrative found also in Joshua 24:15, "Choose the gods whom your ancestors served. . . . But my family and I will serve the LORD."

Throughout Scripture, we find the central role of families not only as the formative entities in youth life but also in the propagation and development of the community of faith. We not only have to help our families understand this precedent but we also have to "re-ingrain" these values into our entire faith community.

Outsourcing Is No Longer an Option

One of the main contributing factors and hurdles in this realignment of faith formation is the prominent role that parental outsourcing has played in our culture. When Johnny wants to learn to throw a baseball, we sign him up for the baseball team; when Suzy wants to learn to dance, we send her to ballet class; when the sink clogs, we call the plumber. We are a culture of specializations. While in some cases these are helpful, in the instance of spirituality, outsourcing is incredibly detrimental. It is also impossible. While we can outsource some things in productive ways, spirituality, whether as an active or passive influence, primarily comes from the parents. So no matter whether the parent is praying with the child each night, makes rude comments about the sermon at Sunday dinner, or proclaims that there is no God at all, that parent has the vast majority's share in the child's spiritual development. By understanding this information, we can help parents recognize that there is no one better suited to lead their child's spiritual development than themselves. We must reimagine our roles not as the primary influencers but as equippers of parents and families as the spiritual nurturing hub of each other within the larger body of the congregation. The outsourcing of our students' faith is no longer an option. The parents' role in their children's spiritual nurturing is just as important as is their role in their children's physical and emotional rearing. We must reaffirm, reequip, and reassert the home as the primary place of spiritual development and growth.

How to Use this Parent's Guide

The parent guide is meant to be used by the youth minister (or someone else who has read the previous chapters) in a small group setting or as informal conversations about spirituality and parenting.

Each of this guide's six chapters coincides with the youth curriculum and has three parts: The first part (Observation, Implication, Application) will, in a simple and concise form, state the data, explore what the data means, and discuss why it matters. The second part has simple talking points for beginning and growing conversations with parents. The third part includes practical "next steps" for the families to take on. Again, this can be used in a small group setting or sent as an e-mail to parents with whom the student minister has had conversation and who want to go deeper. These are not comprehensive or all-inclusive sections but merely starting blocks. These practices should be done in consecutive months, not all at one time. The hope is that this is not a rushed process but one in which parents will be allowed to marinate in and take slowly.

One of the greatest fears of youth ministers, namely having conversations with parents, will be realized in this guide. For many of us, this is scary and often uncharted territory; but it is an adventure on which we must embark. With such a major portion of our youth's faith coming from their parents, we cannot ignore these conversations. My hope is that this guide will that enable you to make that first step, first contact, first conversation toward the shared goal of our youth's faith and spirituality and give you the courage and strength to enter into deep holistic relationships with parents. I hope that it will help you see that you are not only minister to and with the youth but to and with their parents as well. Be strong and courageous. I promise, most of them don't bite.

1: THE MYTH OF NICE

Observation

Our culture has influenced the Church and Christianity in such a way that the radical gospel of Jesus Christ, the one who proclaimed that the first shall be last, who ate with prostitutes and tax collectors, and who told us to love our enemies, has been diluted into a loose set of beliefs, the first of which is that to be Christian is to be nice, be kind, and have the best intentions.

Implication

The message and mission of Jesus has been transformed into a moralistic set of rules that are supposed to make his followers into "good people" by the contextual standards of class, country, and political ideology.

Application

Our churches and youth groups have become "safe" in the worst possible way. We have created a bland, homogenous culture which values "not rocking the boat" more than "stepping out of the boat and walking on water."

The Problem of Being Nice

The primary pitfall for parents in this chapter is that they could possibly understand us as saying that their kids should not be good people. As you begin to have this conversation with parents, it is imperative that they understand that this is not an attack on manners or kindness. It is, however, a discussion about what it doesn't mean to follow Jesus. Following Jesus is so much more than being nice.

Some Talking Points

Jesus said in the Beatitudes that we are blessed when we are lied about and are persecuted because we follow him closely. What would make people persecute us? Some of the things Jesus calls us to do go against our culture and often pushes people out of their comfort zones. "Nice" would tell us to not push the envelope; Jesus seems to constantly push against the accepted norms of our world.

Jesus tells us that when we have enemies, we should pray for them and that when they hit us on one cheek, we should turn the other. This reaction goes way beyond nice. Good people are usually determined by a standard of cultural norms. Jesus calls us to a whole other set of norms, based not on what our contemporaries tell us is OK but on how he lived. These norms involve self-sacrifice, love, and our aligning ourselves with the poor.

People often want the church to be a nice place, as well. When we look at the history of the Church and what Jesus has called the Church to be, we see something very different. We see the Church being called to be a place that causes cultural and societal change. It is a propagator of personal change that is often very difficult and causes rifts among communities, friends, and even families. The Church is a transformative entity in the world. When we ask the Church not to be a transforming body, we ask it to no longer be the Church.

The Practice

One of the greatest things parents can teach their youth is the practice of self-reflection, helping our youth ask the difficult question, the "why" of their actions and beliefs. Asking these questions can do wonders as we strive for the higher calling that Jesus called us to throughout his life.

Spend a month reading sections of the Sermon on the Mount together (Matthew 5–7). A great time to read is around the dinner table every night before eating. Just read a small section of the Sermon and talk about the differences that you see in the text as opposed to how people live. Talk about what is a "good" or "nice" way to act in difficult situations, and then talk about what Jesus, calls us to do. Begin by covering one Beatitude each night, and work through the passages as it makes sense for your family.

Part of this practice also assumes that you will eat dinner together regularly. Do not skip this part. There are countless studies that show the power of the shared meal. The minimum should be four out of seven nights together. This habit will take some sacrifice, but is imperative to begin to reshape the priorities and practices of the Christian family.

2. THE (UN)COMFORTABLE GOD

Observation
Much of the modern Christian's understanding of the church is wrapped up in the idea that God, the Scriptures, and the church's primary purpose is to offer comfort and self-actualization. Contemporary society has created a desire for the church and God to function as a sort of religious genie in a bottle/therapist whose purpose is to boost self-esteem, improve confidence, and help us work through our problems.

Implication
This understanding has taken a gospel whose focus is the reconciliation of the world and has made it about the improvement of oneself. It is has turned an inherently outward focused movement into an inwardly focused and sometimes stagnant group with very little understanding of the fact that we are called to usher in the kingdom of God on this Earth.

Application
Church and youth group can often sound and feel more like a pep rally or a therapy session, instead of being a place that practices

the reconciliation of not only the self but also of the world. We've become focused on our own success.

Why Comfort Should Make Us Uncomfortable

While the Bible is full of stories of God being the great healer, physician, and comforter, the scope of the text is much greater than this image alone. We live in a time and place where much of our focus is on the inward self, its development, and the level of actualization achieved. The inherent goal of this sort of theology is that our youth will be successful people who feel good about their faith and their life. This "theology" often takes a practical form of self-help sermons and programs aimed at making us into happy Christians. The problem is that there is a world that is abused, hurting, starving, war-ravaged, and dying while we, as western Christians, are focused on developing successful lives and worshipping a God who makes us feel good. We find that this is a problem of centrality and focus. Our wants are central, and our well-being and success is our focus. When we move out of our focus on comfort and success and begin focusing on helping others, much of our wallowing in self-fulfillment and success seems much less important because we begin to understand that it is not about us; it is about God's plan and love for the world.

Some Talking Points

When you talk to almost any youth—and many adults for that matter—and you ask them when they felt most aligned with God, the overwhelming answer is on a mission trip. We even talk about it in many youth groups as that "mission trip high." The majority of the time, it is written off as a top-of-the-mountain experience that inevitably fades away as we get farther from the trip. What if that "high" is not because we are in just the right place at the right time? What if it is striking a nerve at the very core of who we are, who God made us to be? Usually these trips are full of hard work, poor sleeping conditions, and situations that are emotionally, physically and spiritually taxing; yet we have a "high." Maybe it is not a high at all but our youth are getting glimpses of the kingdom of God; and they like what they see, especially compared to a world that is focused on them.

Throughout the Bible, we see this constant image of God calling humanity to join with God in the care for creation and one another. The image that is played over and over again is one of the sacrifice of self for the good of everyone else. Nowhere was this on a more prominent display than the very act of literal self-sacrifice of Jesus dying on a cross for the sake of all of humanity.

The Scriptures are often viewed as a 12-step manual or a book of inspirational quotes that help get us through our day. We often read the Scriptures, trying to find something to help us and encourage us to do what we want to do. Instead of reading the Bible as a document in which to find what we need, what if we were to let its words read us and tell us who we are and what God is calling us to become?

The Practice

We as parents often find ourselves playing defense in the ways we raise our children. Sometimes we are so concerned that they will be damaged that we over analyze their lives and end up focusing on our perceptions of their happiness. This action results in an unintended preoccupation with making sure that our children "feel good" about life and all of its elements. As a byproduct of this action, our children see this idea of self-actualization and gratitude as the core of what it means to be fully alive. When we read the Gospels, Jesus paints a much different picture than that of our modern preoccupation with ourselves.

Read Matthew 25:31-46 together as a family. As a family, identify all of the things that Jesus points out that he uses to differentiate the sheep from the goats. Write these on a piece of paper that the whole family can see. Ask yourselves as a family and as individuals how many of these things you have either done individually or collectively over the past year. Be honest; other families are doing this exact same exercise, with just as frustrating results. Now ask yourselves as a family how you can do these more on an individual level as well as a do them as a family.

Each week, have a family check-in with the list you made; and add what you have done as individuals and as a family to fulfill the call that Jesus places to us in Matthew 25. Keep this list somewhere prominent so that it can be a constant reminder of the life that we all are called to as reconcilers of the world.

After a month of keeping the list, sit down as a family and see whether you find any trends in your types of service. Look to see whether there are things, people, or places that your family naturally gravitates toward. When you discover these trends, challenge your family to go a step farther. Instead of having these tendencies be a random part of your daily lives make a plan to research, discuss, and begin at least one element that will be the a focus of your family's energy and time for the entire next month. This component should be something that is challenging, is out of your comfort zone, and is very intentional. Some examples are serving at a homeless shelter together, making care packages for death row inmates, finding and volunteering in an inner city ministry, making dinner once a week for poor or struggling families in your community. After each weekly experience, discuss why this element is a necessary addition and how to live into the saying, "Give a man a fish and you feed him for a day; teach a man to fish and you feed him for a lifetime

3. DEVELOPING A GOOD SET OF GOD GOGGLES

Observation

The majority of our youth and adults practice a form of modern deism that has a profoundly limiting effect on how close God can come, what God can do, and where God can be in our understanding of our lives. This modern deism allows God to come close only when God is needed to solve a problem.

Implication

This notion of the containment, or distance of God, has produced a version of the faith that allows the compartmentalization of different aspects of the Christian life. This compartmentalization has allowed the modern Christian to relegate God and the values of Christianity to certain acceptable areas and has allowed others to exist and to function while void of the intrinsic influence of the Christian faith.

Application

Adults and youth alike make decisions, allegiances, and choices based on hundreds of influences. The problem is that their faith and its primary values and calls are just one of myriad influences. This understanding of the place and prominence of the gospel in our everyday lives leaves Christianity and its influence as just another option in our student's decision-making tool kit, instead of the primary tool by which to live.

With Eyes Wide Open

We have a choice when it comes to God's involvement in our lives and in the world. It is not the choice that we most commonly practice, however. The choice we usually practice is the one that allows us to pick and choose what parts of our lives that God is a part of and function in those parts as we feel that God would have us. This is not the choice at all, however. This is a choice that exists only in our minds. The real choice is not where God is going to be involved in our lives—God is always there; the choice is whether we choose to see, acknowledge, and follow God's lead. When people try to limit God's presence and influence in their lives, they are, in some sense, closing their eyes and pretending that God is not there. We have the choice to live with squinted eyes or with eyes wide open. I usually talk to my youth about the importance of putting on their "God goggles." This is code for reminding them that God is everywhere, working in all things, and that sometimes we have to put on these goggles and be intentional about looking for God in all situations. I am quick to remind youth that this does not mean that God is causing bad things to happen—just the opposite. God is in all situations, even the worst of situations. Instead of God causing something bad to happen, God is working in those situations against the bad and bringing out goodness in the most dire of circumstances.

Some Talking Points

We as parents are some of the biggest culprits when it comes to excluding God from our circumstances and decision-making. One of the ways we exclude God is by not acknowledging God's role and presence in our decisions and goals. If our children think that we are making decisions based only on what we come up with, instead of based on the ethics and priorities outlined by Jesus, then we will inadvertently tell our children to do the same.

When talking with parents, ask how often they are intentionally talking about God in places in their lives that do not involve the church or youth group? Some examples are when the family is setting its budget for the year, when they are discussing politics or watching the news, or when they see someone who is homeless or poor. As parents, we can do such a service to our youth to remind them to constantly put the God goggles back on. We can help them see that God moments are happening all around them.

The Practice

As a family, we have the greatest of opportunities as we raise our children. We have the opportunity to help shape and mold their minds to constantly be looking for the work and involvement of God all around them. This is not only so that they can see God but even more so that they can see where God is working and can join in with God in God's love for our world. I am suggesting one of the most practical, concrete, and family-friendly ways to look for God's involvement around us. This simple, discussion-based activity is another one to do around a meal together.

The practice is called the "Everyprayer." Everyone in the family will talk about God in three categories: everywhere, everyone, and everything. This categorizing is good for the whole family because of its simplicity. Everyone gets to choose one of the three "everys" listed above and talk about either where he or she saw God, in whom he or she saw God, or in what situation he or she saw God. Some examples are: My six-year-old daughter might choose "everything" and say that she saw God in the love that our cat always gives her in the afternoons when she gets home from school. My four-year-old son might chose "everyone" and tell us about how his teacher at preschool helped him learn something new today at school. Whereas my wife might chose "everywhere" and tell about her jog this morning and of seeing the most beautiful sunrise.

The Everyprayer ends with a simple prayer of a family member giving thanks to God for these things we see and the thousands of other things we do not see. This form of devotion and praying is not only an ancient practice of the Church but also helps our children have a part of the theological discussion and helps them practice a theological awareness of their surroundings. This practice will help them go through life not knowing what life is like without God goggles. The byproduct of this practice is also that they will find it much more difficult to compartmentalize God, since they have spent so much of their lives looking for and finding God everywhere.

4. (UN)BECOMING THE CENTER OF THE UNIVERSE

Observation

It is a commonly held belief that teenagers think that they are the center of the universe. It is a common practice that teenagers act as though they are the center of the universe. For all intents and purposes, our teens live life as though they're the only person who exists.

Implication

Our youth practice what I call the two weeks five feet rule. This means that not only do they believe that they are the center of the universe but that their universe has a very small orbit. Commonly this fleshes itself out that they can only see two weeks out and what is happening in a five-foot radius.

Application

Because of this phenomenon, it is very difficult for youth to see the greater picture of the world around them as well as how God is working and calling them to work in that world.

Living Beyond Ourselves

Our youth, like us have the natural inclination to turn inward. The difference in youth and their adult counterparts is that adults have responsibilities that force them beyond themselves (more often than youth do). Paying bills, working in an office or a factory, taking care of children, and so forth cause adults to have to live beyond themselves, to varying degrees. Most youth are learning to take care of just themselves at certain levels. For many parents, if a teenager picks up her room, does his homework and is reasonably clean they consider their teen to be a responsible teenager. Often parents feel, rightfully so, that the job of parenting is so overwhelming and takes so much time and energy that our focus is solely on getting them to be self-sufficient. The problem with this line of thinking is that we are not preparing our teens for a life that does anything but take care of themselves. This is not the life that God has called any of us, adults or youth, to live. We have a responsibility to our youth to make sure that we not only tell our children that they are not the center of the universe but we also have to act toward and treat them like that as well. When we pull them out of that understanding, we help them see that God has called them to something so much bigger—a life of love, sacrifice, helping others, and following God closely. When this awareness happens, they not only realize their place in the world, but they are enabled to live fully into that place and stop living a life of "me, me, me!"

Some Talking Points

I think that this is one of the easiest things to talk to parents about. The majority of parents I talk to are completely overwhelmed with their children's sports, school, homework, extracurricular activities, and so forth. The kids' lives tell them that it is all about them. Their schools', coaches' and instructors' requirements are telling them the same thing. The demand on a family's time is like never before. I am sure that this subject will not have to be explained to very many parents. I imagine that many of them are already talking with you about this pretty regularly. This intense focus on our kids by these entities, and often by parents, helps perpetuate this five feet, two week world.

The Practice

Sit down as a family and ask the question, "What prioritizes and consumes the majority of our 'family time'? This means the non-work, non-school times (after 6:00 p.m. on weekdays and what we do on the weekends)." As you list activities, the most helpful way to think about it is in terms of seasons. If you make a list in three-month periods, it will not only make more sense but will be much more manageable. One of the easiest ways to make a list like this is to give everyone a different color marker and a paper calendar, and have each person write down everything from practices to recitals to business dinners. You'll have a visual representation of what things and which members of the family are consuming the majority of the family's time.

Once you have done this exercise, look at the calendar as a family and decide a few things:

> *When are the really busy times in the year? You will usually find that early fall and late spring are the busiest seasons.*

> *What are things you can cut out?*

> *Is there an overly busy person?*

Look at the times where the calendar is not as busy and think about some family priorities during these times.

Use this time to purge and take away things from your calendar. It will be difficult at first, but you need to make sure to take away enough to calm the schedule but also to be able to add some things that are outside the realm of "me."

Finally, decide as a family how you are going to use your newly balanced schedules to go outside yourselves.

> *How are you going to help others?*

> *How are you going to be involved in your community?*

> *How are you going to take Sabbath?*

> *How are you going to prioritize family worship times?*

> *How are you going to do a family mission trip instead of a vacation?*

> *How are you going to clean up a neighborhood?*

The possibilities are endless. Make sure that these are not token excursions but that they are decided upon by the family, regularly scheduled, and prioritized as you would do baseball practice or piano lessons. Constantly remind the youth that the family is not doing this as an add-on. Help them understand that sports, homework, and extracurricular activities are the add-ons and therefore receive less priority.

Thinking in the prioritizing manner is a huge conceptual shift. Make sure to take it slowly; it's a long process. What you are doing now, intentional family time and helping others, is a central part to your family. Work to develop and ingrain that sense into your teens' understanding of family and personal time management.

5. CONSUMERISM:
THE INSATIABLE HUNGER

Observation

We live in a time in which we are advertised and sold to more than in any other time in history. Recent studies have told us that the most advertised to demographic is our children.[1] The primary technique used in advertising is to make the focus of the advertisement feel as though they have a deficit, need, insecurity or longing that can only be filled by the product being sold.

Implication

Since our youth are the primary focus of the majority of advertising, the message they are receiving is that they are unhappy, needy, and incomplete without buying more stuff.

Application

Our youth consistently want more and more and are trying to feed a hunger that cannot be satisfied. As parents, we want to protect them from the hurt and pain we see in the world; so we give in, buy more, and still feel the same emptiness as before. And the insatiable hunger begins to rumble in our stomachs again.

Taming the Beast

The problem with consumerism is that we are all victims and perpetuators of its power. Our kids see this behavior, and we as parents have guilt because of it. Where our kids want the next generation tech device, we want the newest model SUV. Our kids want the expensive jeans, and we buy more jewelry or the latest television. One of the first steps to curing an addiction is to admit that we have one. Let's all take a big breath and admit that we are addicted to stuff. Say it out loud. . . . good job. Now that we are beyond the easy part, let's move on to the difficult part: I have found it very difficult to talk with people about (our) addiction to stuff. I usually get one of two answers: denial or justification. I don't think that it is our job to guilt people into the idea that we all have a problem with acquiring stuff, but I do think we have to be in very open and honest community-based conversations about this issue. It is not only a problem of being good stewards of resources but also an issue of family strain, priorities, and well-being of our families for generations to come.

Some Talking Points

One of the most helpful ways I have found to begin these conversations with parents is to talk about happiness and satisfaction in their lives. At first, the answer will usually be the same: "We are doing well, the kids are a mess but their grades are good, the (husband/wife) is doing _____ and (he/she) seems to be enjoying that. Thanks for asking!" If, however, we are able to be in continual conversation with people in honest and open ways, we will learn that their lives are not so nice and organized. We will find pain, heartache, dissatisfaction, fear, loneliness, anger, anxiety, frustration, and an overwhelming guilt and fear that they are the only ones who feel this way. One thing that these conversations always seem to come back to is finances, job security, debt, or a desire to "upgrade."

Entering into these conversations is both difficult and time consuming, which is part of the reason that these conversations have to happen in a parent small group. The small group should be people who know that something is not adding up and want to make a change. Unfortunately, this is not a conversation that can be entered into with just any parents. There has to be a common known or understood desire to try something different with their lives or family. If that desire is not present, you can be sure to come up against a lot of push back, anger, and a fight for the status quo.

The Practice

Step 1: Form a small like-minded group (four to six couples) to meet and have dinner together, with the agenda of talking about living in intentionally different ways as a family.

Step 2: When this group meets, tell them up front that this is an opportunity to talk about some of the major issues facing families today and to talk about some ways they as a group think we can face those issues as a Christian community. Tell them that you have put five major issues into a hat; and allow one couple to take one out, read it aloud, and let the group discuss the issue.

Step 3: The issues are parenting, money, dissatisfaction in life, faith, and fear. The couple who draws the topic must speak about it first, then each set of couples speaks about it in turn. After all of the couples have responded, ask these questions of the group:

> *What is the simplest answer to your feelings?*
>
> *Where in Scripture do you see Jesus dealing with these feelings?*
>
> *How do we see these issues reflected in our own children?*

Step 4: Finally, offer that this group is not about getting easy answers to difficult questions but is about getting a group of people together to discuss these issues, to hear and be heard, to commit to journeying together toward some common goals, and to think about doing life together instead of trying to do it all alone. Let them know that you encourage them to continue to meet, discuss, and work together and that you will be more than willing to help them find books or other resources to help their discussions. Leave them with the challenge to discover a new path, to never believe that there are only two answers, and to look for Jesus' third way as they talk.

1. *Branded: The Buying and Selling of Teenagers,* by Alissa Quart (2003).

6. CHANGING THE WORLD
BY LOVING THE WORLD

Observation
We are living in a time of great integration, pluralism and change.
We live in a time and place where different cultures, religions,
lifestyles, and ways of living are interacting with one another more
than ever before.

Implication
With this closeness, not only in knowledge but also in proximity,
the faith of and the way the modern Christian interacts with the
"other" has to be reconsidered and reevaluated unlike ever before.

Application
Adults, youth, and families have to re-navigate what are the core
values of their faith and how those core values cause them to act, to
live, and to treat others whom they believe to be very different than
they are.

Changing the Rules of the Game

We are a competitive people. Our economy, entertainment, politics, and lifestyles are based on who is right or better and who ultimately can win. This line of thought permeates in very deep ways how we understand our religion and faith. It is amazing how Baptist and Methodist churches across the street from each other can bicker and argue as though they were from opposite sides of the universe, when, in fact, they should be loving neighbors. We always want to be the best or at least have others believe that we are the best. The problem is that the way we differentiate ourselves is by propagating the image that everyone else is evil, weak, incompetent, or foolish. We play this game, believing that these are the only rules by which to participate. Jesus calls us into a different way of playing the game, which not only applies to issues of economics and politics; Jesus even calls into this third way of living as we interact with other religions.

Some Talking Points

We do not often, if at all, see Jesus talk about other religions in the Gospels. It's not because he was in any sort of religious vacuum, but because he was surrounded by other forms of Judaism, Hellenistic culture, and many other religions that do not exist today. Jesus was a Palestinian Jew living in a Roman-occupied city under a Roman law. He knew other religions and was regularly exposed to them. It is interesting that Jesus did not take a combative stance against the people who practiced these religions. Instead, he was open to them, helped them, and loved them. Look at the story of the good Samaritan, the healing of the Syro-Phoenician woman's daughter, the woman at the well. These were all people of different religions—even the hated Samaritans—and Jesus' ultimate response was to help and heal each one. When he tells the story of the good Samaritan, he is telling it in the context of how to "inherit eternal life." All of a sudden, how we treat others, even people of another faith, becomes a matter of inheriting eternal life.

Jesus also told us that we should be known by love. Throughout the Gospels, he tells to love our neighbor, turn our cheek, and pray for our enemy. He even tells us in the Gospel of John, "I give you a new commandment: Love each other. Just as I have loved you, so you also must love each other. This is how everyone will know that you are my disciples, when you love each other." (John 13:34-35) We are constantly being told by Jesus to love, not based on religious affiliation or denomination or faith at all; but because we are Christians, we will love.

The Practice

Learn: In the age of blogs, 24-hour news, and e-mail forwards, it is all too easy to be fed a lot of false information about others, especially people of different faiths. In order to better understand and consequently not function with misconceptions, we have to learn about our brothers and sisters of other faiths. One form of this knowledge is through books: literally learning the tenets of their faith, their practices, history, and contribution to the world. This knowledge can come from a variety of sources, not the least of which are temples, mosques, and other places of worship. You have to begin with one religion, focus on it, and then explore from there. The second part of the learning cycle is to learn from real followers of that faith: meet, talk with, and even share a meal with people of other faiths. This action can be very difficult for many people who live in places that feel like mono-religious communities. If you look, you will be able to find some who practice other religions. If not, find a larger city close to you and see whether their (I hope) more diverse community has any places of worship you can visit. Another great inroad to meeting people of other faiths is food festivals. Often people of other faiths or from other countries will participate in food festivals displaying their culture; art; and often times, their faith. Just in my city alone, there are nearly ten of these festivals every year.

Work: We are different in so many ways. We also have so much in common with people of other religions. We have many of the same hopes and dreams, problems, and heartaches. There is so much we have in common. A wonderful way for families to understand this commonality is to find common goals with people of other faiths and work on achieving these together. Community restoration, helping the poor, and celebrations are all things we can do together. Having common goals and purposes allows people who otherwise would never talk to one another to work and build foundations of trust together. After these foundations are built, so many other avenues exist to travel together, each based in a common trust, hospitality, and love for other.

Love, Hospitality, and Good Samaritan-ism: These three Christian principles are vital when developing relationships and understanding with people of different faiths. Have your family sit around the dinner table and read the story of the good Samaritan together. Identify everything the Samaritan did for the Jew. Talk with your children about how we treat friends, strangers, and even enemies. Do we treat them the way the Samaritan treated the stranger and enemy on the road? Make a list of the way people talk about and act toward people of other religions. Is this the way the Samaritan treated the person on the road? Finally, write a family covenant together. This covenant should be an agreement by the family on how you will treat friends, strangers, and enemies. The outline of this covenant should come from Jesus' words on love, the story of the Samaritan, and how we are to treat our enemies. Hang this covenant by the door so that you will be reminded of it every time you leave your house.

Because good youth ministry doesn't just happen

In today's world, good youth ministry requires more than just games and guitars.

Whether you're a **youth minister** who wants training or a **church** in need of a stronger youth ministry, the Center for Youth Ministry Training is here to help.

For youth to experience a life-changing faith, they need an intentional community of teens and adults where they have a personal encounter with God, are encouraged to understand God's purpose for their lives, and find home in the intersection of their story with God's bigger story.

For this kind of youth ministry to happen, both youth workers and churches need training.

The Center for Youth Ministry Training brings together **Partner Churches** and **youth ministers** to create life-changing youth ministries through our **Graduate Residency in Youth Ministry**.

For more information on the Center for Youth Ministry Training Graduate Residency program or to learn more about other CYMT resources visit www.cymt.org.

CPSIA information can be obtained
at www.ICGtesting.com
Printed in the USA
LVOW04s1707031115

R10185900002B/R101859PG460513LVX4B/1/P